Hands on a School Year

Liz Webster and Sue Reed

Acknowledgements

The publisher and authors Liz Webster, Headteacher of Aldingbourne Primary School, and Deputy Headteacher Sue Reed, would like to thank all the children and staff of their school for their enthusiasm, hard work and cooperation in the creation of this book. They would like to especially thank Wendy Davies and Kath Herbert for their hard work and dedication, and Saffron Ancell for his/her photographs of children in the Art Club, some of which have been included in this book.

Both Liz Webster and Sue Reed would like to express a special thanks to their partners, Phil and Ollie, whose support and patience has been invaluable. Finally, they would like to thank Steve and Alison Forest, the photographers, for their consistent help and understanding.

Published by Collins
An imprint of HarperCollins*Publishers*
77–85 Fulham Palace Road
Hammersmith
London
W6 8JB

© HarperCollins*Publishers* Limited 2013

10 9 8 7 6 5 4 3 2 1

ISBN 978 0 00 748939 8

British Library Cataloguing in Publication Data
A Catalogue record for this publication is available from the British Library

Cover design by Linda Miles, Lodestone Publishing Limited
Internal design by Linda Miles, Lodestone Publishing Limited
Photography by Elmcroft Studios
Edited by Liz Miles
Proofread by Gaynor Spry

Printed and bound by Printing Express Limited, Hong Kong

Browse the complete Collins catalogue at
www.collinseducation.com

MIX
Paper from
responsible sources
FSC™ C007454

Contents

Introduction

In every primary school classroom around the world, seasons, festivals and other important dates are celebrated by children with help from their teachers. This book aims to show how you can celebrate these notable dates through a creative, dynamic and, above all, fun approach. It also shows how you can make the most of these opportunities to provide your children with invaluable learning experiences.

What do we mean by a 'school year'?

Whatever your nationality, there are certain dates in the year that will be celebrated by your community. Some of these will be traditional dates that are steeped in history and have long been celebrated in this way, such as Harvest, Easter or Pancake Day. Others will be dates celebrated in order to teach children about diversity and religious experiences or communities that are unfamiliar to them. These might include the USA's Independence Day, the Thai Songkran festival or the Spanish bull-run festival in Pamplona.

Hands on a School Year is, of course, not suggesting that you teach all of these events! The book offers suggestions of how you might turn any of these dates into informative and fun-filled cross-curricular lessons for the children. The book is packed with ideas for you to use with your class and to adapt to suit your own school calendar.

How can I use *Hands on a School Year*?

Throughout the book we have demonstrated that the most effective lessons are practical and exciting for the children. Each chapter offers a range of stimulating and original ideas that we use in our classrooms – so we know they work!

Every theme in this book follows the same basic structure – with a whole-class starter, practical activities, ideas for art and display, and cross-curricular links.

Whole-class starter

The whole-class starter aims to introduce the theme to the children, making it exciting, meaningful and relevant to their lives. Each whole-class starter includes some helpful background information as well as ideas for exciting teaching strategies to engage the children. Teaching strategies include the teacher in role and visual props such as the use of an interactive whiteboard (IWB).

Practical activities

These include class, group and paired work, for example lively games and children working with a partner to discuss ideas and experiences.

Art and display ideas

Hands on a School Year focuses on using art and display as a means of making your learning as visual as possible in the classroom. Each theme includes suggestions for ways in which children can express their ideas through a range of art activities. These activities encompass all art skills from painting to collage and from sculpture to textiles.

Each theme includes at least one high-quality classroom display, chosen to reflect a huge range of different ways to display the work. The displays in the book have been chosen to inspire you with:

- imaginative ways of creating lettering
- a variety of different colour schemes
- the use of backing and borders for effect
- ways of using a large focal point in a display
- methods for creating captions, key words and questions
- ways of displaying the children's work.

We believe that displaying children's work is not only important to celebrate the children's achievements and give the work value, but also acts as an invaluable way of visually reinforcing the children's learning.

Cross-curricular links

We have highlighted ways in which links can be made between different times of the year or festivals and other curriculum areas to help learning become more relevant and meaningful for young children. If used imaginatively and comprehensively, the school calendar can provide a gateway to all other aspects of learning.

Liz Webster and Sue Reed

Halloween

Whole-class starter

- Using birthdays as an example, talk to the children about what we mean by a celebration. Ask the children if they can think of any other celebrations. What special things do they do on those days?

- Introduce the celebration of Halloween by telling the original *Meg and Mog* story by Helen Nicoll and Jan Pieńkowski. You could put witches' clothes on (such as black shoes, cloak and hat) while explaining that, one day, Meg puts on her witches' clothes to go to a Halloween party with other witches. Continue the story, describing how the witches put ingredients into Meg's cauldron, and finishing with a Halloween spell.

  - Describe what you need for your spell, dropping a word card for each item into a cauldron:

  - A date – explain the date for Halloween is always 31 October. Historically, this was regarded as the last day of summer.

  - Witches, devils and fairies – explain that witches, devils and fairies come out on Halloween because it is their annual holiday.

  - Pumpkins, lanterns and bonfires – explain the old custom of making pumpkin lanterns and fires to ward off evil spirits, and how we still make lanterns today.

- Parties – explain how Halloween parties traditionally involve dressing up and playing games such as 'Bob Apple'.
- Trick or treat – explain how the tradition of 'Trick or treat?' is the most popular part of Halloween today with children and their parents going from door to door in fancy dress in search of treats.
- A name – explain that the word Halloween comes from All Hallows' Eve, and that Hallows means saints. Halloween is celebrated in many countries around the world.

Whole-class practical activity

- To check the children have remembered the information, play 'Who Wants to be a Millionaire?' asking questions about Halloween. If a child gets an answer wrong, they have to drink some witches' potion!

Art and display

The following project ideas show a variety of tasks that can be completed to explore Halloween through a selection of collage and painting techniques.

- **Spooky Pumpkin Art:** Paint a large pumpkin and add collage use black paper or ink to create a spooky Halloween character.
- **Colour-mix Pumpkins:** Colour-mix different shades of orange, and paint a pumpkin-shaped piece of paper to show depth and shadows.
- **Collage Pumpkins:** Draw three different-sized pumpkins with chalk pastel cut them out and place on a green background. Add leaf detail.
- **Cauldron display:** Use paints and collage to create a large witch and cauldron for display.
- **Witchy Hands:** Help the children to draw round their own hands. Use oil pastels to extend the fingers and make witches' hands.
- **Halloween Hands:** Add a Halloween symbol such as a ghost, a pumpkin, a bat, etc. on each finger of children's hand outlines. Use pen and pencil crayons to add colour and detail.

Cross-curricular links

Design and Technology: Read and enjoy Jan Pieńkowski's pop-up story *Haunted House*. Design and make a pop-up page.

Literacy: Read the story *Meg and Mog*, focusing on the adjectives used to describe the witches' clothes.

Literacy: Play 'Witchy Words', with the children wearing witches' hats. Pull pictures of witchy items, such as spiders, frogs, hats and broomsticks, from a card cauldron. The children write as many adjectives as possible to describe each item within a given time. Give a treat to the child who has the most adjectives.

Diwali

Whole-class starter

- Talk to the children about what a festival is (a time of celebration). Tell them that some festivals are very well known and celebrated widely, while some are less well known and only celebrated in certain places. Explain that many important festivals are linked to religions.

- Discuss the religion of Hinduism with the children. Explain that Hinduism is the religion of most of the people in India. In England many families with roots in India follow the Hindu religion. Explain that Hindus worship at temples and they believe that after death a person will be reborn – perhaps as an animal. Discuss with the children which animal they would like to be if they were reborn.

- Explain that for Hindus one of the most important festivals is Diwali, also known as the festival of light. It celebrates the victory of good over evil, of light over darkness.

- Talk about traditional Diwali celebrations. Diwali homes are filled with gaily-coloured lights, people clean their homes and give each other presents. Lamps are lit and traditional Hindu dances are performed. In India, streets are decorated with lights and sparkling fireworks are lit.

Whole-class practical activities

- Invite the children to tell you a fact about Diwali. For each fact given, light a tea-light in celebration of the festival of Diwali.

- Play 'Light-up'. Give each child a laminated board on which several lamps are drawn. Pre-prepare a bag of true and false statements and one picture of someone blowing out a lamp or candle. Encourage children to take turns to pick out a statement from the bag. If the statement is true they can draw a flame on one of their lamps. If false, they miss a go. If they pick out the card with the picture of somebody blowing a candle out, they must rub out all their flames. The winner is the child who has drawn all their flames (lit all their lamps).

Art and display

These ideas use a wide range of media, including textiles, to create Diwali candles and lamps. Some or all can be used to create a Diwali Display of Light.

- **Textile Candles:** Encourage the children to create a Diwali lamp image using a collage technique (fabric or paper). Add glitter for the flame.

- **Diwali Word Candles:** Using the word Diwali, turn each letter into a candle or lamp. Use watercolour pencils to add colour.

- **Perspective Art:** Focus on perspective by asking the children to draw a Diwali lamp, then repeat but with the lamp viewed from a greater distance. Use chalk pastels.

- **Diwali Lamp:** Using oil pastels, draw and colour a vibrant Diwali lamp.

Cross-curricular links

Dance: Invite the children to learn a typical Hindu dance.

Drama: Retell 'The Story of Diwali' using props.

RE: Research the Hindu patterns known as Rangoli. Create or copy a Rangoli pattern using a pencil crayon to draw and felt-tipped pens to add colour.

Science: Investigate the importance of light. How does light travel? What is a light source? What materials allow light to pass through them and what materials don't?

Science: Explore the Northern Lights phenomenon. Watch video clips of the Northern Lights, then recreate the images using calico, oil pastels and a fabric paint.

Guy Fawkes Day

Whole-class starter

- Explain to the children that fireworks are lit in most countries during festivals and celebrations. In England, it is traditional to have fireworks and bonfires on 5 November.

- Tell the children that today they are going to explore the reasons behind the celebration of the Gunpowder Plot, when Guy Fawkes and a group of men tried to blow up the Houses of Parliament in 1605, using barrels of gunpowder hidden in the basement. They were trying to kill King James I because they wanted the laws against Roman Catholics to be changed. Soldiers found the plotters and the King ordered a huge bonfire to be lit in celebration. Show the children an old 'dusty' book as a prop (use talcum powder for the dust). Explain that it's a history book which tells the story of Guy Fawkes. Open the book and blow the 'dust' from the page. Tell the story.

- Finish the lesson by showing images of Bonfire Night and fireworks. Discuss the children's experiences and the different kinds of fireworks they have seen.

Whole-class practical activity

- Play 'Hot Potato Fire Words'. Using a 'Hot Potato' game, the children must pass the 'hot potato' (a beanbag works well) around the class. Each time the potato is given to a child they must call out a firework word. For example: fizzle, bang, pop, crackle, etc.

Art and display

You can select from the following art and display ideas to focus on bonfires, fireworks, or on the story behind Bonfire Night.

- **Guy Fawkes Story:** Use pen and inks to draw a scene from the story of the Gunpowder plot.

- **Colour-mix Flames:** Colour-mix shades of red orange and yellow on a flame-shaped piece of paper. Display the flames together to make a bonfire.

- **Flame Movement:** Create a bonfire scene with oil pastels. Use a video clip to show children the movement of flames close-up that they can feed into their work.

- **Firework Scene:** Drop watered-down paint onto paper and use a straw to blow it into firework shapes and create a firework scene.

- **Night Sky Collage:** Use ripped tissue paper to create a collage night sky with fireworks.

- **Felt-tip Fireworks:** Use felt-tipped pens to draw firework images, filling the piece of paper with colours.

Cross-curricular links

Literacy: Write a firework poem. This could be written in firework shapes such as a Catherine wheel.

Music: Create a song about fireworks to the tune of 'Ten Green Bottles' (e.g. There were ten big fireworks standing in a line, … and if one went ZOOM and exploded in the sky…). Play musical instruments to add atmosphere.

PSHCE: Discuss firework safety and teach The Fireworks Code.

Monkey Buffet Festival

Whole-class starter

- Explain to the children that some of the less well-known festivals, in the UK and around the world, are very unusual, such as the Turnip Festival, Redneck Games Festival, Tomato Throwing Festival, Baby Jumping Festival and the Mud Festival!

- Introduce and explain the unusual-sounding Monkey Buffet Festival. It is held every November in the city of Lopburi in Thailand. It does not have any religious roots but celebrates the local monkey population, which lives in the city and has adapted to city life. The festival centres around a huge buffet of fruit and vegetables for the monkeys to enjoy. People from all over Thailand, as well as foreign visitors, come to feed the monkeys and enjoy the festivities. Thousands of kilograms of fruit and vegetables are donated to the monkey population, with the hope that this generosity will bring good luck to the people.

Whole-class practical activity

- Using pictures saved onto the interactive whiteboard, share and discuss images of the Monkey Buffet Festival with the children. Organise the children into pairs and give each pair a laminated speech bubble. As a picture appears on the interactive whiteboard, ask the pairs to fill in a speech bubble for one of the monkeys or people, and share them with the group.

Art and display

As well as developing a wide range of art skills, these project ideas can be used to help children learn about many different fruits and vegetables.

- **Monkey Art:** Paint a watercolour background. Using paint and collage, create monkeys in different poses for display.

- **Fruit Art:** Using real fruit and vegetables for reference, draw large pictures of them using chalk pastels.

- **Fruit and Monkey Collage:** Create a fruit or vegetable background for a collage of a monkey. You could use wrapping paper with fruit designs to collage the monkeys.

- **Fruit and Vegetable Monkeys:** Create a monkey out of oil pastels, using fruit and vegetables in place of different parts of their body, such as bananas for the tail.

Cross-curricular links

Geography: Research other festivals in Thailand. Learn about traditions and customs in Thailand. Find Thailand on a globe.

PSHCE: Discuss the origins of the saying: 'See no evil, Hear no evil, Speak no evil.' Why are monkeys used? What is the saying trying to teach us?

Science: Learn about lots of different types of monkeys and their characteristics.

St Andrew's Day

Whole-class starter

- Tell the children that you are the ghost of Saint Andrew. You lived in the time of Jesus and you were one of the first people to follow Jesus. Explain that you witnessed Jesus perform miracles such as when he fed a crowd of thousands with just five loaves and two fishes.

- Explain that you were a Christian but were killed for your beliefs. However, your story had a happy ending as the man that looked after your grave had a dream and in his dream an angel visited him and told him to take your bones somewhere safe and beautiful. The man travelled the world far and wide until he came to Scotland and thought it perfect! The King was so kind that he dedicated a church especially for the burial of your bones. The place became known as St Andrews and is still there today. St Andrew's Day is celebrated every year in Scotland on 30 November.

- Tell the children that, in your role as Saint Andrew, you will teach the children everything you know about Scotland. Display and explain large pictures on the interactive whiteboard: the Scottish flag, the national flower (thistle), St Andrew's golf course (one of the oldest in the world), Scottish dancing (reel or sword dancing), clans, bagpipes, castles, haggis, tartans, kilts, shortbread, Nessie, etc.

Whole-class practical activity

- In role as the ghost of St Andrew show a series of items or images, some of which are Scottish (such as a kilt) and some of which are not (such as daffodils). Every time the children see something Scottish, they must perform the Highland fling!

Art and display

Scottish customs and culture can be explored to create a 'Scotland' display.

- **All Things Scottish:** Give each child a letter from the word 'Scotland' and ask them to create a design based on Scottish customs. Put them together for a 'Scotland' display.

- **Thistle Art:** Use chalk pastels to draw a thistle on black card.

- **Bagpipes and Nessie:** Use chalk pastels to create large, colourful images of Scottish culture.

 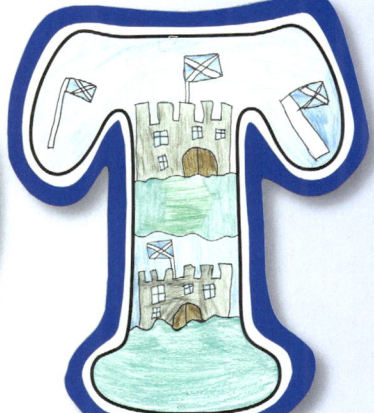 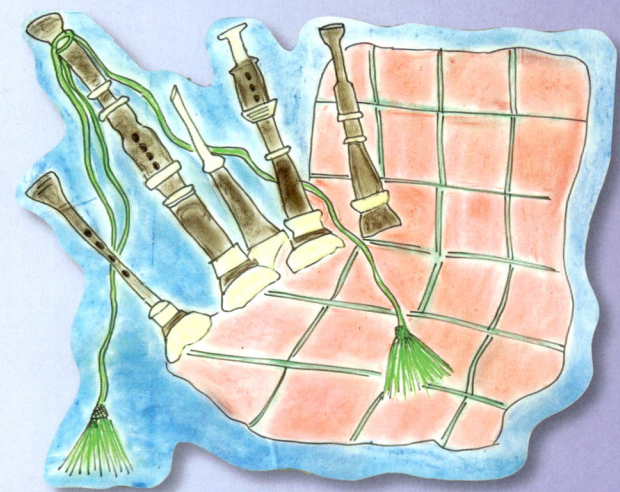

Cross-curricular links

Art: Using a weaving technique, design your own Scottish kilt.

Design and Technology: Bake shortbread biscuits.

Literacy: Learn about the legend of the Loch Ness Monster and then ask the children to write their own Nessie adventure story.

Literacy: Spend time studying Shakespeare's 'Scottish Play' (*Macbeth*). Ask the children to design and make their own poster advertising the play.

PE: Hold your own Highland Games with caber tossing (a long roll of corrugated card), hammer throwing (a ball in a sock or a quoit on a piece of string). Learn a traditional Scottish dance for the Games.

Hanukkah

The display board text (handwritten):

- anukkah is celebrated around the world for eight days and nights.
- Nine-branched candleabrum, known as the Menorah is lit during the week of Hanukkah.
- ovember or December are the months when the festival of Hanukka might take place.
- sually Hanukkah is a time when families eat latkes and sufganiot to celebrate the miracle of the festival of Light.
- islev is the Jewish month in which Hanukkah begins.
- hanu is the Hebrew word for Hanukkah, meaning 'and they rested.'
- toy, known as the dreidel is played by children during Hanukkah week.
- anukkah is the story of a great victory of the Jews over the Syrian-Greeks.

Speech bubble labels: What is a dreidel? How long does the festival of Hanukkah last? What type of festival is Hanukkah? What is the importance of Kislev? Why is 'Hanukkah' known as the miracle festival? What is the Menorah? What traditions do families do to celebrate Hanukkah? In which months could Hanukkah take place? What is the Hebrew word for Hanukkah? What type of festival is Hanukkah?

Whole-class starter

- Explain to the children that Hanukkah is a Jewish festival, also known as Chanukah or the Jewish Festival of Lights. To explain more about the festival, use the eight letters in Hanukkah as an acrostic poem.
  - **H**annukah is celebrated around the world for eight days and nights.
  - **A** nine-branched candelabrum, known as the menorah, is lit. The central candle is used to light the other eight candles, with one additional candle being lit on each of the eight days of the festival.
  - **N**ovember or December is when the festival of Hanukkah takes place. Sometimes it crosses through from one month to the other.
  - **U**sually Hanukkah is a time when families eat latkes (potato pancakes) and sufganiot (deep-fried doughnuts), or other foods fried in oil, to celebrate and commemorate the miracle of the Festival of Lights.
  - **K**islev is the Jewish calendar month in which Hanukkah begins.
  - **K**hanu is the Hebrew word for Hanukkah, meaning 'and they rested'.
  - **A** toy, known as the dreidel, is played with children during Hanukkah week. It is a four-sided spinning top with a different Hebrew letter on each side.
  - **H**anukkah commemorates the Jews' struggle for religious freedom.

Whole-class practical activities

- Play 'Hints about Hanukkah'. Give each child a board with eight words or images linked to Hanukkah. On the interactive whiteboard present the children with one question at a time about Hanukkah. They must choose a word or image from the board that answers the question. The children tick the correct answer on their board.

- Share with the children the sequence in which the candles on the menorah are lit. The candles are lit from left to right but the newest one to be lit is put on the far left, so that the candle from the first night of the festival is not always lit first, which might make it seem more significant than the others.

Art and display

These ideas are based around the powerful image of the menorah, to contribute to a Hanukkah display.

- **Colour-wash Candles:** Use a wax crayon to draw the nine candles you would find on the menorah. Add a yellow flame and add a colour wash over the top to create a wax resist background.

- **Collage Menorah:** Use a variety of wrapping paper to create a colourful collage of a menorah.

- **Finger-paint menorah:** Use bright paints to finger-paint a menorah on a black card background.

- **Tree menorah:** With watercolour pencils, draw a tree to represent a menorah.

- **Symbols of Hanukkah:** Create a chequered background using different shades of blue paint and wrapping paper. With gold and silver pens, add symbols linked to Hanukkah in selected squares.

Cross-curricular links

Design and Technology: Make potato latkes or Hanukkah candy.

History: Research the life of the Jewish people through history. Find out about the life of Anne Frank. Why were the Jewish people persecuted in World War II?

Maths: Investigate the 'answer is 9'. Ask the children to find as many sums as they can in which the answer equals 9.

Maths: Draw the Star of David. What mathematical facts can children find in their drawing?

Christmas Around the World

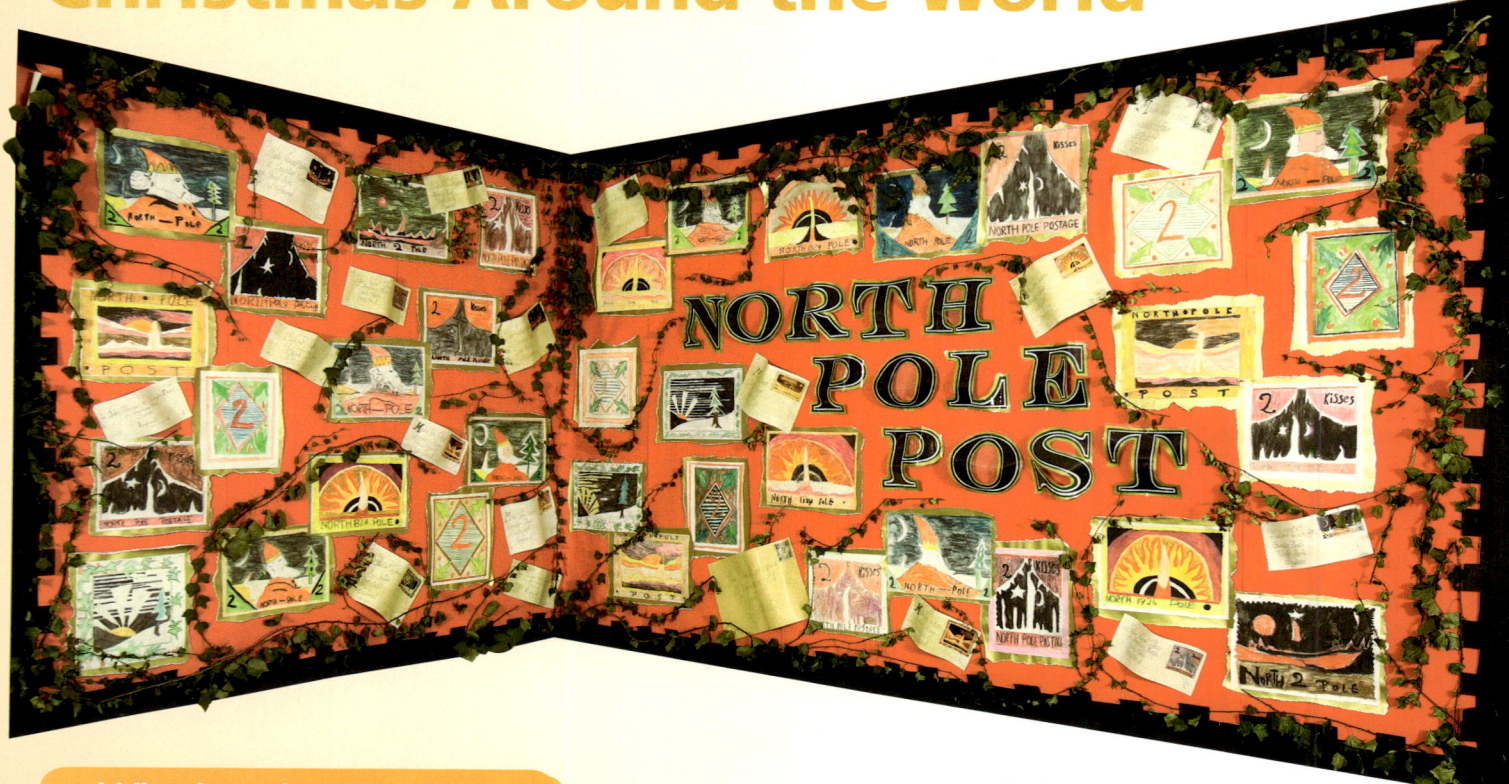

Whole-class starter

- Prepare a postbag full of letters ready for when the children arrive. Each letter should reveal information about the Christmas traditions in a particular country, such as Australia, France, Greece, India, China and Bethlehem. An example of a letter from Italy is shown on the right.

- Make sure the children are aware that Christmas is the festival celebrating the birth of Jesus Christ. It is increasingly celebrated in non-Christian countries.

- Tag the postbag with a note: 'Ho, ho, ho! To show you how Christmas is celebrated around the world, read some of the letters written to me from children all over the world! Love from Santa xxx'.

- Read the tag to the children and then pick one letter out at a time and read it to the children.

Dear Babbo Natale,

Buon Natale! We are so excited about Christmas here in Italy. We decorated our house yesterday and our nativity scene looks beautiful on the windowsill. I am going out with other children this evening to sing carols door-to-door. I hope I will earn some treats for my singing! I am not looking forward to fasting for the 24 hours before Christmas Eve but it will be worth it when we have our Christmas feast. I'm especially looking forward to my favourite – the pannetone! I'm even more excited about being visited by La Befana, the kind old Christmas witch on the Epiphany! I hope she fills my stocking with toys for being good, and not coal!

Love from Carlo

Whole-class practical activity

- To revise the facts they have learnt, ask the children to sit in a circle and give each child an envelope with a fact about how Christmas is celebrated in a particular country. For example, 'In this country people decorate mango and banana trees to celebrate Christmas.' (India) Put hoops (labelled with the countries they have learnt about) in the centre of the circle. Play some Christmas music while the children deliver their fact to the correct hoop.

Art and display

The following project ideas can be used to contribute to a display focused on Christmas in different countries.

- **Christmas Stamps:** Draw Christmas stamps and paint with watercolours.

- **Globe Art:** Draw a globe with watercolours and add Christmas motifs around the edge to represent different Christmas traditions.

- **Wrapping-paper Flags:** Using Christmas wrapping paper, create a collage of flags from around the world.

- **Santa's World:** Use felt-tipped pens to draw and colour a large A3 Santa with the world as his stomach.

- **International Christmas:** Create the word 'Christmas' by drawing letters and colouring each one as a different country's flag.

Cross-curricular links

ICT: Ask the children to research Christmas traditions in a variety of countries.

Languages: Investigate how to say 'Merry Christmas' in different languages.

Literacy: Share and discuss a range of Christmas stories from around the world.

19

Christmas

The display board shows various Santa-themed children's artwork with speech bubble questions:

- Why does Santa have a beard?
- Where does Santa live?
- Who leads Santa's sleigh?
- Why does Santa wear big boots and gloves?
- What is Santa's real name?
- What does Rudolph like to eat?
- What colour coat does Santa wear?

HO HO HO!

Whole-class starter

- If possible, enter the classroom in role as Mrs Santa (or Santa), carrying a prepared sack containing hidden items related to Santa, such as a red coat, a red hat, black boot, beard, red nose, bell, sack, carrot and gloves. Explain to the children that your husband is famous all over the world, and that in some countries he is known as Santa, in other countries St Nicholas or Father Christmas. No matter what he is called he does the same job every year. He brings happiness to children by delivering lots of lovely presents.

- Still in role, explain that there has not always been a Santa, and you want to tell them the true story of Father Christmas. Tell the story of St Nicholas and how he helped a poor father from having to sell his three daughters. He sneaked into the house and left money in stockings so that they could afford food and would not have to be sold. He then continued to help poor people in his village. The news spread about these mysterious kind acts in the night, but nobody ever knew who it was – just like today!

- Explain that over time Santa has changed and now needs a lot of help and special equipment to do his job correctly. Take items from your sack and ask the children if they can identify what each item is.

Whole-class practical activity

- Play 'Mix and Match'. Laminate different Santa objects and cut each into two pieces to create jigsaw style shapes. Give each child a piece of a jigsaw. Play Santa music while the children find the child with the shape that matches theirs. Once they have found their match ask each child to say what the item is and to explain its importance.

Art and display

These ideas use all sorts of different media, both 2D and 3D, to create Santas for classroom display.

- **2D Santas:**
  - Draw a felt-tipped hand outline and turn it into a Silly Santa.
  - Use chalk on black card to create a St Nicholas picture.
  - Finger-paint Santa's face on a blue background.
  - Create a Santa using a handprint for his beard and add a paper hat. Finger-paint his face and add big eyes.

- **3D Santas:**
  - Create a Santa collage using a doily and paper for his head. Finger-paint a snowy background.
  - Make a Santa collage with ripped paper.
  - Paint a Santa face on a large pebble to create a paperweight.
  - Create a collage of a fat Santa using a variety of festive wrapping paper.
  - Make a Santa hat on a parcel paper background. Use scrunched red tissue paper and add cotton wool. Use pens to create a stitched effect around the edge.
  - Make clay Santa tiles.

Cross-curricular links

Design and Technology: Make Christmas Santa biscuits.

Design and Technology: Using a range of construction materials, make a correctly-sized chimney for a laminated Santa. Use the Santa picture to check he will fit.

Literacy: Write an acrostic poem using the letters of SANTA.

Literacy: Write a thank-you letter to Santa.

Maths: Investigate 3D shapes, using Santa presents of various shapes, such as cube, cuboid, sphere, cylinder, cone and pyramid. Investigate which shapes are easy to transport on his sleigh.

Maths: Children cut out and stick 2D shapes to make a Santa.

Chinese New Year

Whole-class starter

- Explain to the children that Chinese New Year occurs on the first day of the first month of the Chinese calendar, that it is an important time for family reunions and is also known as the Spring Festival. Make a chart comparing New Year celebrations in Europe or the USA, with Chinese New Year celebrations. Look at both similarities and differences.

- Discuss the 12-year cycle and the use of animals to represent each year. Each animal is one of the 12 Chinese Zodiac signs, and is associated with different characteristics. The order is: Rat, Ox, Tiger, Rabbit, Dragon, Snake, Horse, Goat, Monkey, Rooster, Dog, Pig. If children know what year they were born in, help them to find the animal symbol.

Whole-class practical activities

- Sit the children in a circle. Place 12 hoops in the middle of the circle and place a picture of one of the 12 Chinese New Year animals in each hoop. Give each child a card with a characteristic of one of the animals written on. On a given signal, the children place their cards in the correct hoop. Discuss the children's choices.

- Play 'Chinese Chase'. Give 12 children a bib with an animal picture pinned on the front. The other children wear bibs displaying words that describe the animals, such as 'woolly coat' (sheep) and 'fiery breath' (dragon). The object of the game is for the 'animals' to chase and catch the words that characterise their animal. Repeat several times.

Art and display

As well as, or instead of, creating a Chinese New Year display, children can really enjoy creating Chinese lanterns.

- **Decorated Years:** Ask the children to choose an animal and the year it will next feature in the Chinese calendar. Print the year out using a large font. The children draw images related to their chosen animals and colour with pencil crayons.

- **Chinese Plates:** Give each child a paper plate. Ask them to choose an animal and, in the style of Chinese art, the children draw their animal. Use Chinese decorative art to fill the gaps on the plate.

- **New Year Animals Display:**
  - Use chalk pastels to draw the 12 Chinese New Year animals.
  - Ask children to write words that characterise these animals, to add to the display.
  - Write a title in the style of Chinese writing.

- **Chinese Lanterns:**
  - Make a Chinese lantern using cellophane and wire.
  - Ask children to use the wire to create an image that appeals to them and attach it to a stick.
  - Cover the wire in cellophane.
  - Use paint to create detail.
  - Attach an artificial tea-light inside the wire image.

Cross-curricular links

PE: Play 'Chinese Twister'. Create a board with lots of words that characterise the Chinese New Year animals. Make two spinners: one with an instruction, such as left foot, right foot, and one with New Year animal names. The children take it in turns to spin both spinners and carry out the instructions when their animal comes up.

PSHCE: Discuss with the children 12 animals they would choose as New Year creatures and why.

Valentine's Day

Whole-class starter

- Discuss with the children when Valentine's Day is (14 February) and ask them what they know about this special day. Give each child a heart-shaped sticky note and ask them to write one fact about Valentine's Day on it. Place the notes on the board and discuss.

- Tell the story of St Valentine, the priest who lived in Rome around AD300. Explain that he was killed by the Romans for giving shelter to persecuted Christians. At the same time, the Romans were celebrating a festival of love, also known as Lupercalia. Because of Valentine's kindness and the time of his death, Valentine became known as the patron saint of lovers.

Whole-class practical activity

- Discuss some of the traditions or beliefs linked to Valentine's Day, such as the old superstition that the first unmarried man a girl sees on Valentine's Day will be her future husband. Ask the children if they know any Valentine's Day traditions. Create a mind map to display their ideas.

Art and display

There are two sets of ideas here – one using heart-shaped cushions and one for making a display of hearts created using different art techniques.

- **Colour-mix Hearts:** Colour-mix reds and pinks to create different shades. Use them to paint a heart-shaped piece of paper.

- **Valentine Collage:** Use strips of Valentine-themed wrapping paper to make a collage. Glue it onto a heart shape torn from an A4 red sheet of paper.

- **Oil Pastel Hearts:** Using oil pastels draw hearts in different sizes and colours. Put onto a black background.

- **Word Art:** Draw the word 'LOVE', in a 1960s hippy style, using watercolour pencils. Decorate with drawn hearts.

- **Heart Cushions:** Sew a heart cushion using felt. Add sequins and embroidery for detail. Use all the cushions to create a class display.

Cross-curricular links

History: Find out who the Greek goddess of love is.

Literacy: How many other words can the children think of that have the same or a similar meaning to the word 'love'?

Literacy: Write a love poem to someone. Make it anonymous. Use this structure:

> Roses are red
> Violets are blue
> Sugar is sweet
> and so are you!

Science: Learn about the heart. Why is the heart important and what is its main function? Draw a heart diagram showing how the heart pumps blood around the body. What protects the heart? Investigate what happens to the heart when we exercise. Listen to each other's heart using a stethoscope.

Pancake Day

Whole-class starter

- Ask a teacher or assistant to enter the classroom dressed as a chef. Explain that the chef has come to teach them all about Pancake Day – a special, traditional day – and that a chef is the most qualified person for the job because he or she knows all the correct ingredients for a perfect Pancake Day!

- Get out a frying pan and add ingredients (key words on laminated pancakes) as the chef 'cooks up' a Pancake Day:

  - A special name – explain that Pancake Day is known as Shrove Tuesday.

  - A time of year – explain that Pancake Day is always in February or March and it is 47 days before Easter Sunday.

  - A tradition – explain that it is traditional on this day to eat pancakes. These are thin cakes made in a pan using flour, milk, butter and eggs. Games and pancake races are also traditional and lots of fun!

- A reason – explain that it is the last day before a period of time which Christians call 'Lent' – a Christian festival leading up to Easter Sunday. Lent is a time of abstinence, of giving things up. So Shrove Tuesday is the last chance to be indulgent, and use up the foods that are not allowed during Lent. Pancakes are eaten on this day because they contain the forbidden foods: fat, butter and eggs.

- Friends around the world – explain that Pancake Day is celebrated all over the world by Christians and has many different names. In France they call it Mardi Gras, which means 'Fat Tuesday'. In Iceland the day is known as Sprengidagur (Bursting Day).

Whole-class practical activity

- The chef stirs the ingredients to make a perfect Pancake Day, then pulls out of the pan one paper pancake at a time. Show the children activities pre-written on the back, which they will take part in as part of their Pancake Day. The chef reads them out, saying: 'Today on your perfect Pancake Day, you are going to…
  - make pancakes
  - toss pancakes
  - race with pancakes
  - enjoy a pancake story
  - do pancake sums.'

Art and display

Here are some ideas for a Pancake Day display. Display it on a 'tablecloth' if possible.

- **Giant Chef:** Paint and collage a giant chef for the centrepiece.
- **Pancake Day Activities:** Display photos of the children doing their different Pancake Day activities and arrange in groups.
- **Compound Picture Art:** Paint giant compound word pictures. Add them to the display with their corresponding compound words.

Cross-curricular links

Design and Technology: Make, toss and eat pancakes!

Literacy: Read, discuss and retell the story of *Mr Wolf's Pancakes* by Jan Fearnley.

Literacy: Learn about compound words e.g. pan-cake, lady-bird, hand-bag, foot-ball. Make giant jigsaw pieces with pictures on related to compound words. Play pairs to match the pictures and make new compound words.

Maths: Learn to halve and quarter pancakes, shapes and numbers.

PE: Hold pancake races using thick, tacky-backed pancakes. Children run with a pancake in a frying pan to a cone and have to toss the pancake before running back.

St David's Day

Martyn Evans is a famous Welsh Artist.

He was born and brought up in the coal-mining valleys of Wales.

He was inspired by the beauty of the valleys where he was born.

Evans presents the Welsh mining valleys as colourful places of hope.

We used watercolour pencils to create pictures in the style of Martyn Evans.

Daffodils are traditionally worn on St David's Day.

Wales is part of the United Kingdom and the island of Great Britain.

Cardiff is the capital city of Wales.

Saint David is the patron saint of Wales.

St David's Day falls on March 1st.

The red Welsh dragon is the official animal of Wales.

The leek is one of the traditional emblems of Wales.

The daffodil is the national flower of Wales.

The national sport of Wales is rugby.

Whole-class starter

- Explain to the children that today is a very special day in a certain part of the United Kingdom. Using props or an interactive whiteboard display show the children items connected with Wales (for example, a leek, a daffodil, a rugby ball and a dragon) and ask them if they can guess the special day. Explain that the special day is St David's Day and it is very important in Wales and for Welsh people on 1 March.

- Discuss with the children the importance of each item displayed. For example the leek is a national emblem in Wales and is worn on St David's Day, and the daffodil is the national flower.

- Re-tell the story of 'St David and the Leek'. Explain that this story reveals how a monk became known as St David and is now the patron saint of Wales. The story begins during a battle where the two sides became mixed together and it was difficult to tell who was on which side. The fact that both sides wore similar clothing made it all the more confusing. A monk noticed the problem. As the Welsh lost more and more ground, the monk cried out to them, 'Welshmen, you must mark yourselves so that you can better tell who is Saxon and who is Welsh.' The monk pulled a leek from the ground and urged, 'Wear these so you will know that any soldier who does not have a leek is your enemy.' Some of the soldiers thought this was a rather odd idea, but they trusted the monk so they agreed. Soon every Welsh soldier was wearing a leek on his helmet. They attacked their enemies and before long, the Welsh had won the battle. The monk's name was David. He became known as St David, and he died on 1 March, which then became St David's Day. The leek is also the national emblem of Wales and is worn on St David's Day.

Whole-class practical activity

- Play 'Leeks or Daffodils'. For this game you can either use real leeks and daffodils or make two sets of laminated picture cards, one set of daffodils and one of leeks. Create a set of questions for the children to answer based around St David's Day. Divide the children into two groups. Nominate a captain for the daffodil team and a captain for the leek team. The captain picks a child from their team to answer a question. If they are correct the captain gives them either a daffodil to hold or wear, or a leek, depending on which team they are on. The winner is the team holding the most leeks or daffodils.

Art and display

Different Welsh traditions can be explored to create a display to celebrate St David's Day. The illustrations of Welsh artist Martyn Evans are an excellent source of inspiration.

- **Welsh Daffodil Art:** Using the ripped paper technique and colours from the Welsh flag (red, white and green), create a daffodil image.
- **Sketched Dragon Art:** Using sketching pencils, draw a Welsh dragon, focusing on shading to represent light and dark.
- **Dragon Sculpture:** Use clay to create a Welsh dragon.

- **Welsh Dragon Art:** Create a picture of a Welsh dragon with felt-tipped pens. Place it on a green and white background to represent the Welsh flag.
- **Daffodil Field:** Using chalk pastels, create a picture of a field of daffodils.
- **Dragon Collage:** Collage a Welsh dragon onto a chalk pastel background.

Cross-curricular links

Design and Technology: Make leek and potato soup or Welsh cakes.

Geography: Study Welsh landmarks. Show the children pictures of famous landmarks, for example Severn Bridge, Cardiff Castle, Mount Snowdon, etc.

Languages: Learn to say 'hello' and 'goodbye' in Welsh. If possible, learn a Welsh song.

Holi

Whole-class starter

- Explain to the children that today they are going to learn all about the Festival of Holi. Holi is a festival celebrated in North India and Nepal by Hindus. It is a fun-filled festival that marks the coming of spring, and is usually in March.

- Tell the children the legend of Holika and Prahlad. Prahlad was a prince. His father, the King, wanted everyone in his kingdom to worship him. But Prahlad refused and worshipped Lord Vishnu instead. The King's sister Holika, who was supposed to be immune to fire, tricked her nephew Prahlad into sitting on her lap in a bonfire in order to destroy him. But because she was using her powers for evil, the plan failed and Prahlad emerged from the fire unharmed, while Holika was devoured by the flames. Explain that the story of Prahlad is seen to symbolise good overcoming evil and because of this bonfires are traditionally lit at Holi. In some parts of India effigies of Holika are burnt on the fire. In other parts of the country, roasting grains, popcorn and coconuts are thrown onto the bonfire by Hindu families. Ashes from Holi bonfires are thought to bring good luck.

- Some people also believe the origin of the festival lies with Krishna, who was very mischievous as a young boy and threw coloured water over the *gopis* (milkmaids). This is why, although some families hold religious ceremonies, for many Holi is more a time for fun and it's traditional to celebrate the festival by playing practical jokes and games. Holi is a colourful festival, with dancing, singing, and people throwing powder paint and coloured water. Everyone gets involved and Hindus of all ages have great fun splashing and smearing each other with paint – all in the spirit of celebration!

- To conclude the lesson, play a slideshow of images of the Festival of Holi, with appropriate Hindu music playing in the background.

Whole-class practical activity

- Discuss primary and secondary colours. Teach the children how to colour mix the seven different colours of the rainbow using the primary colours. Learn how to mix many different shades of each colour.

Art and display

The Festival of Holi centres around colour. The following ideas ask children to play with colours and can all contribute to a 'Happy Holi' display.

- **Collaged Handprint Picture:** Using bright colours, ask the children to make lots of handprints. Once dry, cut out and create a collage.

- **Hand Shapes:** Ask children to draw around their own hand or a template. Using watercolour pencils and felt-tipped pens, add lots of bright colours.

- **Colours Collage:** Using a ripped paper technique, create a brightly coloured collage of colour splodges.

- **Handprint Art:** Chalk-pastel a multi-coloured background. Add handprints on top.

- **Title Art:** Colour-mix triangles of different colours and use them for the title of the class display.

- **Border Art:** Use leftover handprints to create a display border.

- **Splodge Art:** Chalk-pastel a multicoloured background. Use very runny paint and a straw to add colour splodges all over the background. Add handprints.

Cross-curricular links

RE: Explore aspects of life in India and find out about Hinduism as a religion.

Science: Investigate colour by making a colour wheel-spinner. Investigate how, as you spin it, the colours merge and become white. Investigate separating sunlight into the different colours of the rainbow using a prism.

St Patrick's Day

Whole-class starter

- Explain to the children that St Patrick is the patron saint of Ireland and that he is famous for bringing Christianity to Ireland. He was born in Wales around AD385, then carried off by pirates and spent six years in slavery before escaping and training as a missionary. The most famous story about St Patrick is that he drove all the snakes out of Ireland. St. Patrick's Day marks his death on 17 March AD461. Tell the children all about St Patrick's Day. Explain the importance of St Patrick's Day in Ireland and how it is celebrated as a special day. Include information on the national flag, the importance of the shamrock and Irish traditions.

Whole-class practical activity

- Play 'Share your Shamrock'. Make a set of shamrock-shaped cards with a statement about St Patrick's Day on each. Include statements that are both true and false. Place the shamrocks around the school or classroom area. Invite the children to find a shamrock and bring it back to the carpet. Discuss whether the facts are true or false. Place the true shamrocks on the board and throw away the false statements.

- In Ireland the number three is regarded as a magic number and the three leaves that make up the shamrock are supposed to bring good luck. The three leaves also represent the Trinity in the Christian religion. Ask the children to get into groups of three and give each group a large shamrock-shaped sheet of paper. Ask the children to work together to draw a symbol that represents Ireland or St Patrick's Day on each shamrock leaf. Share with the class.

Art and display

The shamrock shape is an easy one for children to have lots of fun with. You can use some or all of these ideas – and children can offer their own ideas too!

- **Collaged Shamrock Picture:** Cut shamrock shapes out of tissue paper or green wrapping paper, and overlap them to create a collage.

- **Painted Shamrocks:** Using shades of thick green powder paint, and adding sand to give texture, paint a large shamrock onto black card.

- **Shamrock Art:** Cut and stick three different green shamrocks onto white paper. Using green felt-tipped pens, follow the shape of the shamrocks.

- **Abstract Shamrocks:** Using oil pastels draw and pastel a large shamrock in shades of green. Add a multi-coloured background to give an abstract effect.

- **Dynamic Shamrocks:** Draw a shamrock-shaped outline and use felt-tipped lines to fill the leaves with dynamic designs.

- **Display Title:** Cut out shamrock-shaped paper. Use powder paint to colour-mix shades of green. Add a letter for the title onto each shamrock.

Cross-curricular links

Design and Technology: Make some Irish soda bread.

History: Tell the story about Finn MacCool and the Giant's Causeway.

Maths: Invite the adding adder (a snake puppet) into the classroom. Explain that he is very good at adding, and today he is going to help the children add their numbers together. Learn to count in 3s; practise your 3 times table; add three numbers together; and practise adding and subtracting 3-digit numbers.

Easter Traditions

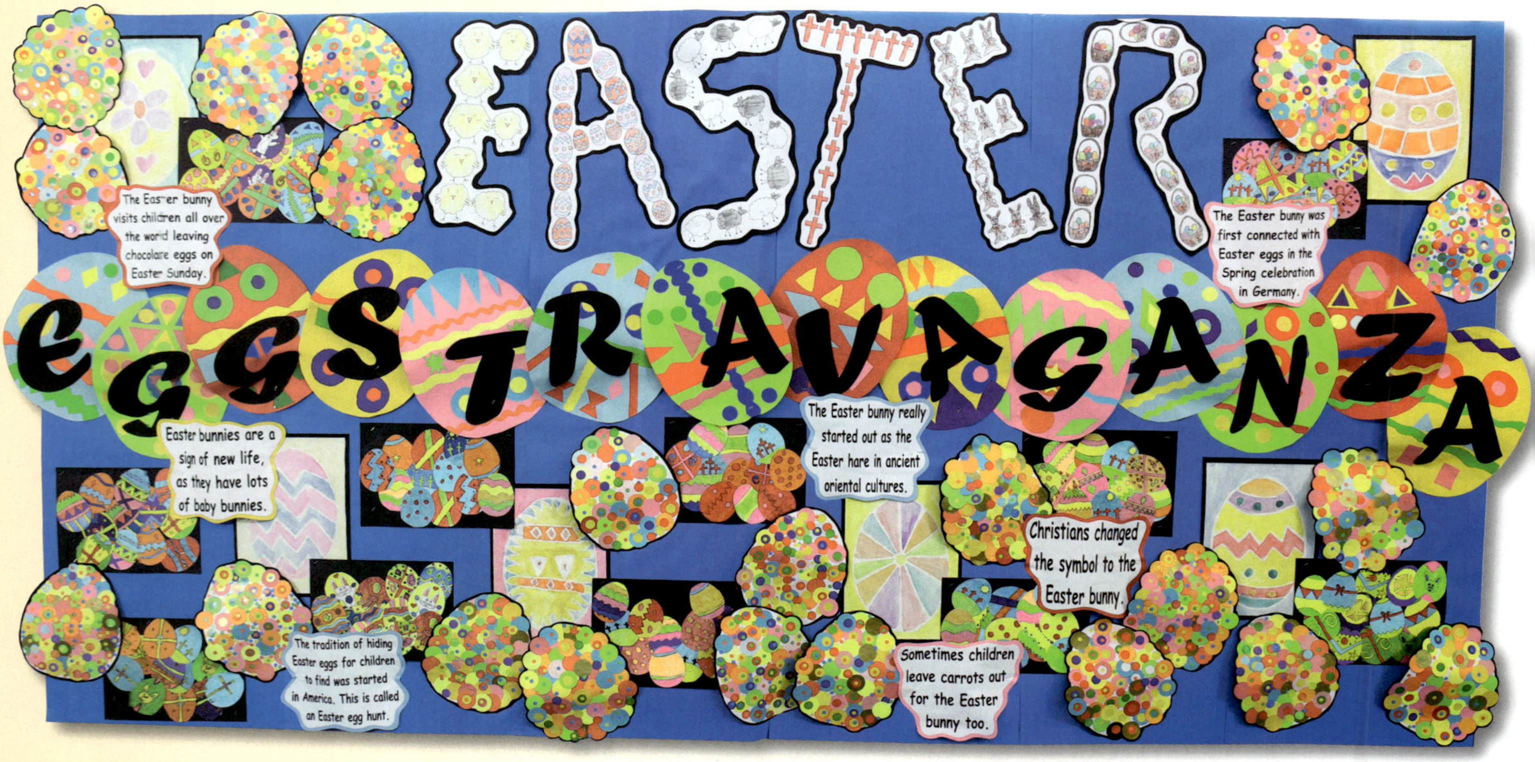
EASTER
EGGSTRAVAGANZA
The Easter bunny visits children all over the world leaving chocolate eggs on Easter Sunday.
The Easter bunny was first connected with Easter eggs in the Spring celebration in Germany.
Easter bunnies are a sign of new life, as they have lots of baby bunnies.
The Easter bunny really started out as the Easter hare in ancient oriental cultures.
Christians changed the symbol to the Easter bunny.
The tradition of hiding Easter eggs for children to find was started in America. This is called an Easter egg hunt.
Sometimes children leave carrots out for the Easter bunny too.

Whole-class starter

- Role-play the Easter Bunny and explain that you have come to tell the children about Easter traditions. Pre-prepare an Easter egg hunt, writing facts about Easter traditions on eggs for the children to find. Encourage the children to search for the eggs around the school and then to share the facts they have found with the class.

Whole-class practical activity

- In role as the Easter Bunny, tell the children that you would like to share some of your Easter eggs with them, but they are not normal eggs and they all have different names. Ask the children if they can guess the names of the eggs. On the interactive whiteboard, show a picture of an egg dressed like a scientist and tell the children his name is Eggsperiment. Show a picture of an egg jumping out of an aircraft: His name is Eggstreme. Ask the children to guess the name of some more eggs. Can they think of their own new eggy words?

The first Easter Bunny was in fact an Easter Hare in ancient oriental cultures.

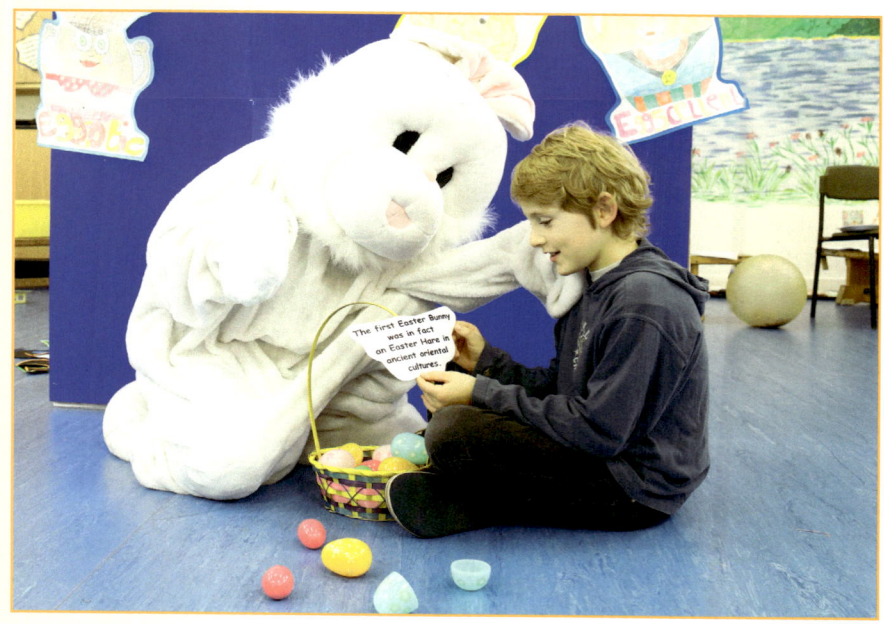

Art and display

As well as using a range of different mediums to create eggs for an Easter display, children can add their fun 'eggy' words pictures.

- **Dotty Eggs:** Use a variety of pre-cut circles to collage a bright Easter egg.

- **Eggy Collage:** Draw Easter eggs and add different patterns using felt-tipped pens. Next, cut out them out and arrange them on black card to create an Easter egg collage.

- **Patterned Eggs:** Give each child an egg-shaped card. The children use cotton buds or art straws to create patterned Easter eggs. Or they can use watercolour patterns to paint Easter eggs in pastel shades.

- **Comedy Eggs:** Using an eggy play on words (e.g. eggsplorer, eggshausted), create comedy eggs with pencil crayons.

- **Eggy Tree:** Brightly decorate lots of hard-boiled eggs and hang them from a tree.

- **Easter Titles:** Create the word 'Easter' for your display title by drawing different symbols of Easter in letter shapes to spell out the word. You can also make giant eggs by collaging patterns and shapes onto egg-shaped pieces of paper, then add letters for an 'Eggstravaganza' title.

Cross-curricular links

Design and Technology: Design and make an Easter bonnet. Organise an Easter bonnet parade around the school playground.

Design and Technology: Organise an egg sculpture competition using eggy words as inspiration. The children must create a model using real eggs to create the word, for example eggstinguisher could be a model of an egg that has turned into a fire.

Literacy: Prepare an Easter egg hunt around the school. Invite the children to find the clues and solve the puzzle of the Easter Bunny's name.

Maths: Using a cuboid net, create an Easter basket; decorate it and place chocolate eggs inside.

The Easter Story

Whole-class starter

- Discuss with the children the importance of Easter to Christians. Do they know why it is the most important day of the year to many people? Ask them to discuss this with a friend. Share their ideas. Explain that it is a time of great happiness and rejoicing and symbolises new life, a new beginning.

- Retell the Easter story using drama and props. Explain to the children that Easter is not just about Easter Sunday but is a whole week, known as Holy Week. Explain that during this week several things happened to Jesus – that he died on the cross, was buried and then rose from the dead. Tell the story and let the children re-enact the events of Holy Week.

Whole-class practical activities

- Create a 'Who Wants to be a Millionaire?' quiz about the Easter story. Children could use whiteboards to reveal their answers.

- Using the interactive whiteboard, create a slideshow on the interactive whiteboard of statements about the Easter story. Give the children a paddle with a red side and a green side. If the statement is correct they show the green side of the paddle. If incorrect they show the red side.

Art and display

There are two display possibilities suggested here – one for the traditional Easter story and one based on creating different images of the cross, in both 2D and 3D.

- **Easter Story Display:** Draw the Easter story using chalk pastels. This could be done individually or in groups and for a large-scale display.

- **Tree Crosses:** Draw a tree in the shape of a cross, adding roots in different shades of the original colour. Explain that the roots symbolise new growth. Use water-colour pencils to add colour.

- **3D Crosses:** Create a 3D cross. Use thick paint to create a background and score cross shapes in the paint while wet. Leave to dry. Cut out a cross shape from card and decorate it with vibrant patterns using oil pastels. Here it is the bright colours that celebrate life. Attach the cross to the background using a polystyrene block to make it stand out.

- **Chalk Pastel Crosses:** Use a template to cover a white cross shape on a large piece of paper. Draw outward marks in a range of brightly coloured chalk pastels. Peel the template away to leave the white cross shape at the centre.

- **Silhouette Crosses:** Create a sunset background using ripped tissue paper in shades of orange and yellow, and glue. Use black to paint silhouettes of the crucifixion scene.

Cross-curricular links

Design and Technology: Learn to make traditional Easter foods: hot-cross buns or simnel cake.

Design and Technology: Design and make an Easter garden.

RE: Research the importance of the cross. What does it symbolise?

RE: Read extracts from the Bible that tell of the events of Holy Week.

Songkran: Water Festival

Whole-class starter

- Explain to the children that today they are going to learn all about the festival of Songkran. It is a Buddhist festival that takes place in Thailand. Traditionally, it is known as the Water Festival and takes place in April, which is the hottest time of the year in Thailand. Using a slideshow presentation explain some of the facts about this fun-filled festival, for example:
  - Songkran is traditionally celebrated as Thailand's New Year and takes place from 13 to 15 April.
  - The most well-known tradition of the Songkran festival is throwing water.
  - Thai people believe that throwing water brings good luck and prosperity for the New Year, that it cleanses the soul and removes any bad actions or thoughts.
  - People visit local monasteries and pay respect to the Buddha by gently pouring water over images of the Buddha.
  - Some people make New Year resolutions, such as to refrain from bad behaviour, or to do good things.
  - Besides washing household Buddha images, many Thai people give their home a thorough clean.
  - Fragrant herbs are sometimes added to the water that is used for cleansing Buddha images.
  - Nowadays, the emphasis is on fun and water-throwing rather than on the festival's spiritual and religious aspects.

Whole-class practical activity

- Play 'Splat or Splash?' Using the interactive whiteboard, create a board with words and pictures linked to the Songkran. Divide the children into two teams. Give each team the opportunity to answer a question relating to the Songkran Festival. They must 'splat' (give) the correct answer. However, if they are incorrect the team gets a 'splash' of water (a spray from a water pistol or clean plastic bottle).
- Show the children images of the Songkran Festival.

Art and display

The following project ideas can be used to create a display that includes both the Buddhist festival and the watery theme of the festival.

- **Water Drop Art:** Focus on colours from the Thailand flag (red, blue and white) and create ripped paper water droplets.

- **Songkran Water Scene:** Oil-pastel small images of people onto a blue paper background. Lightly wet the paper and drop watery paint onto the paper. The paint will spread to give the effect of thrown water.

- **Buddha Art:**
  - Oil pastel a Buddha image using bright colours and an abstract style.
  - On a round sheet of paper draw an image of the Buddha in brightly-coloured felt-tipped pens.
  - Encourage the children to use a printing tile technique to create a tile of a Buddha image. Children use two shades of one colour to print the background and then the Buddha image on top.

Cross-curricular links

Geography: Discuss water conservation with the children. Create a water conservation leaflet giving advice on how to save water.

RE: Research and learn all about Buddhism. Where did it begin? Which are the main countries where people practise Buddhism? What are the main features of the Buddhist religion?

Science: Learn all about the water cycle.

St George's Day

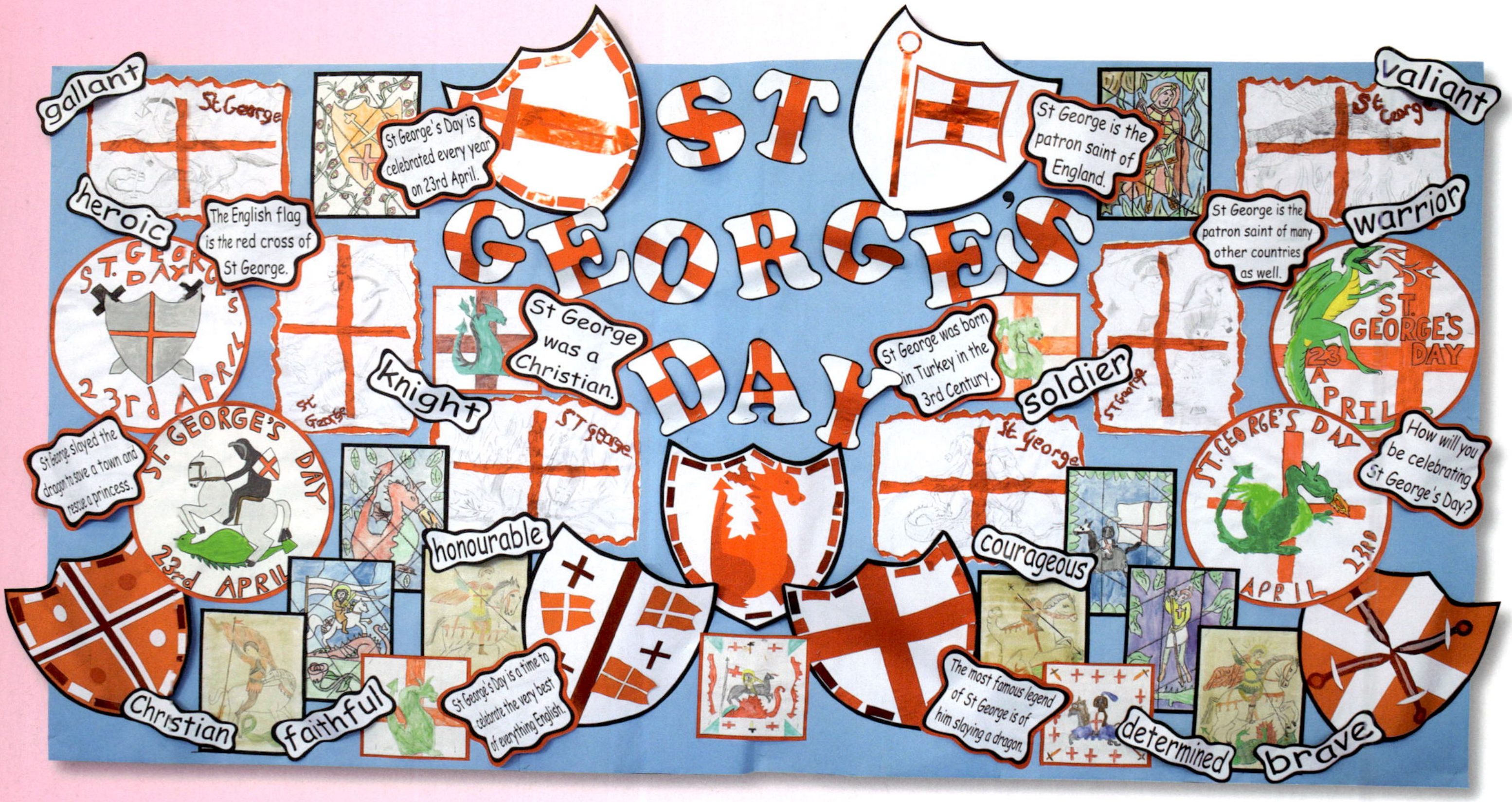

The display board shows various St George's Day themed artwork with the following labels and text:

- gallant
- valiant
- heroic
- The English flag is the red cross of St George.
- St George's Day is celebrated every year on 23rd April.
- St George is the patron saint of England.
- St George is the patron saint of many other countries as well.
- warrior
- knight
- St George was a Christian.
- St George was born in Turkey in the 3rd Century.
- soldier
- St George slayed the dragon to save a town and rescue a princess.
- How will you be celebrating St George's Day?
- honourable
- courageous
- Christian
- faithful
- St George's Day is a time to celebrate the very best of everything English.
- The most famous legend of St George is of him slaying a dragon.
- determined
- brave

Whole-class starter

- Role-play St George and explain to the children that today is a very special day. It is St George's Day and on this day everybody celebrates your greatness. Explain that there are lots of symbols linked to you. Ask them to guess which (from a selection) relate to you, St George. Give each child a laminated sheet with a variety of symbols and images related to St George, plus some images that do not relate to him (e.g. 23 April, rose flower, St George's flag, church, dragon, etc). Ask the children to circle the pictures that relate to St George. Discuss their choices.

Whole-class practical activity

- In role tell the children that you have not always been famous and your story began a long time ago, when you were a Roman soldier who died because he believed the Romans should stop persecuting Christians. Tell the traditional story of 'St George and the Dragon'. With children and props, re-enact the story. This could also be told using an interactive whiteboard with images and sound.

- Play 'Jousting George'. You will need a selection of quoits, cones, two trikes, two long poles to act as jousting sticks and two knight's helmets. Divide the children into two teams and place each team in the corner of the room or large space. Give the first team member the jousting stick, trike and helmet. Ask the two team members a question, such as: What day is St George's Day? The first person to answer the question correctly can have a go at jousting! They must pedal their trike to a cone and pick the quoit up with their jousting stick successfully to win a point. The winning team is the team with the most points at the end of the game.

Art and display

These project ideas take a range of symbols associated with St George as their focus.

- **Title:** Create a display heading using the theme of St George's cross. Cut out white letters and place a red cross on each letter.

- **St George's Shield:** Design and make St George's shield, using a red and white theme. Add images related to St George's Day using felt-tips. Children can make a 'real' shield, or create a collage.

- **St George's Stamp Art:** Draw and colour (using watercolour pencils) a huge St George's Day postage stamp to commemorate St George's Day.

- **Story Sketch:** Sketch an image that depicts the story of St George and the Dragon. Add a red cross of scrunched up tissue paper and the name 'St George' to the image.

- **Olde Worlde St George:** Use damp tea-bags to give an A4 sheet of paper a parchment effect. Draw a picture of St George on his horse. Add colour using pencil crayons.

- **Stained Glass Window Art:** St George is often seen on stained glass windows in churches. Look at some examples and ask the children to draw an image that symbolises the life of St George. Add colour using watercolour pencils. Use a black oil pastel to create the stained glass window effect.

Cross-curricular links

Drama: Divide the children into groups of five. Provide them with the essential props needed to produce a play that tells the true tale of St George and the Dragon.

History: Research St George's coat of arms. Ask the children to either copy or design their own coat of arms.

Literacy: Read and enjoy *George and The Dragon* by Christopher Wormell. After reading the story ask the children to create a story map that retells it.

PSHCE: Organise and hold a St George's Day celebration in school. Allow all the children to come to school dressed in red and white clothes and engage in fun-filled traditional activities.

May Day

Whole-class starter

- On, or close to, 1 May role-play the May Queen. Explain how for hundreds of years 1 May has been celebrated as the first day of summer. Ask the children to talk to their partner about what kinds of things we do to celebrate May Day. Then, in role as May Queen, use large pictures and keywords in an interactive whiteboard presentation to teach the children about May traditions, such as May fairs, maypole dancing and Morris dancing.

Whole-class practical activity

- Use a real maypole or make a temporary maypole using a netball post and ribbons. Ensure that you have enough ribbons for each child. Prepare a set of cards with true/false statements about May Day based on the points from your presentation, such as: May Day is the first day of autumn (false), May Day was once known as Robin Hood's Day (true). Divide the children into two teams (e.g. inner/outer ribbons, red/blue ribbons). Each team should take it in turns to pick a statement. If the statement is true, they can move one place forward, if false they move one place back. The first team to get back to the start wins!

Art and display

These project ideas incorporate the traditional celebration of May Day as the first day of summer, to create a 'May Day Mayhem' display.

- **Maypole Ribbon Art:** Create a sky background using chalk pastel. Use tissue paper to make a collage maypole with ribbons swirling in the wind.

- **Collaged Maypole:** Sponge white clouds onto a blue background. Use strips of paper to depict the maypole.

- **Maypole Scene:** Use a combination of chalk and oil pastels to depict a maypole scene with the focus on drawing children dancing around the maypole.

- **Watercolour Maypole:** Using watercolour pencils draw a maypole and add flowers to the ribbons to symbolise the month of May.

Cross-curricular links

Dance: Learn and perform a maypole or country dance to 'Greensleeves'.

Drama: Create a play based on a Robin Hood adventure.

Literacy: Create a May Day acrostic poem.

Literacy: Compose a May poem or carol ('carol' originally meant a song for dancing).

Solstice

(display board photograph titled "SOLSTICE at STONEHENGE" with children's drawings of Stonehenge and captions)

Whole-class starter

- On the longest day of the year (the summer solstice), you or an assistant could enter the classroom in role as a scientist. Tell the children that today is the longest day of the year and that you are going to explain why.

- Use a globe and a map to explain to the children that:
  - The Earth moves around the Sun.
  - The Earth spins on its axis.
  - The Earth's axis is tilted which means different parts of the world experience different patterns of daylight hours.
  - The summer solstice is the longest day of the year in the northern hemisphere.
  - When it is the summer solstice in the northern hemisphere, it is the winter solstice in the southern hemisphere.

- Explain to the children how lots of people around the world celebrate the summer solstice by watching the Sun come up. Show the children images of sunrise at Stonehenge and explain how every year at this ancient site many people gather to celebrate the summer solstice. It is a huge stone monument built about 5,000 years ago – no-one knows exactly why.

- Discuss how at the summer solstice, it may still be light outside at bedtime. But at the winter solstice it may still be dark when you get up in the morning! Ask the children to mind map activities that they can do when the days are long, and those they cannot do when the days are short (for example go on a bike ride after school, eat supper in the garden). Write their answers on the whiteboard.

Whole-class practical activity

- Use drama to consolidate the children's learning. Choose a child to stand in the middle of the room and pretend to be the Sun. Choose another child to represent the Earth and ask them to hold the globe. Ask the 'Earth' to walk around the 'Sun', counting a year each time the 'Earth' has gone completely around the 'Sun'. Then ask the 'Earth' to spin the globe as they go around the 'Sun' and explain that this is what happens every 24 hours.

- Explain that the Earth is tilted on its axis. Show the children how for one half of the year the northern hemisphere is tilted slightly towards the Sun and at the same time the southern hemisphere is tilted away from it. During this time, countries in the northern hemisphere have more hours of daylight than the ones in the southern hemisphere. The summer solstice is the longest day, when we have the most hours of daylight - in the northern hemisphere this is in June. Explain that, when it is the summer solstice in Britain, it is the winter solstice in Australia.

Art and display

Stonehenge is the stimulus for this display. You can use different mediums and techniques to create very different pieces of Stonehenge art.

- **Sunrise Stonehenge:** Use thick card and create a sunrise background using crayons. Cut and stick stone-shaped card onto the background to depict an image of Stonehenge. Colour the card black.

- **Sunset Stonehenge:** Look at photographs of sunsets and shadows at Stonehenge and create an image of Stonehenge at sunset with chalk pastels.

- **Sketched Scene:** Use sketching pencils and shading to create a Stonehenge scene.

- **3D Stonehenge:** Using clay, create a 3D image of Stonehenge.

Cross-curricular links

Design and Technology: Ask the children to create their own Stonehenge using building blocks.

Literacy: Read and discuss *A Midsummer's Night's Dream* by Shakespeare as your class reader for the week.

Maths: Make a zigzag seasonal book based on times of the day in the summer and winter, drawing the different activities they might be doing at each time depending on the season. For example, at 4pm in the summer they might be at the beach but at 4pm in the winter they might be inside playing a game or watching television.

Science: Hold a 'Solstice Quiz'. In advance, prepare two laminated circles and two sets of six 'sun rays' for each circle. Split the group or class into two teams. Each team takes it in turns to answer questions about the summer solstice and if they get an answer correct, they collect a ray for their Sun. The first team to collect six rays is the winner.

Father's Day

Throughout this topic remember that some children in the class may have an absent father or mother, or there may be sensitive issues linked to either or both parents. Adjust the lesson accordingly.

Whole-class starter

- Display photographs of your own or another's father using the interactive whiteboard. Recall things you used to do with your dad when you were growing up, and talk about what makes him special.

- Explain to the children that it is always important to thank both our parents or carers. Explain that on Mother's Day in March we say thank you to our mums, and on Father's Day in June it is equally important to say thanks to our dads. Ask the children to think about one thing they like about their dad. Using a jingle ball sit the children in a circle and pass the ball amongst the group. When they have the ball they must say what is special about their dad.

- Read and share the book *My Daddy is a Giant* by Carl Norac. Discuss with the children the fact that not all dads are the same. Some go to work and some don't. Some are tall and some are not. Some dads like football and some like gardening. Discuss with the children what makes their dad special.

Whole-class practical activity

- Using the initial letter 'd', ask the children to think of as many words as they can to describe their daddy (for example: daring dad, delightful dad, dopey dad, etc.). Encourage each child to write their word on a sticky note for display on the board. Talk about the children's choices as a class.

Art and display

Even making Father's Day cards can provide the opportunity for a bright classroom display.

- **Father's Day card:** Children could make a card for a story character's dad rather than a real dad, if that is more appropriate. They could use an ICT drawing package to draw a picture of the dad's face and shoulders, then print out. Use oil pastels to paint a colourful pattern on a tie-shaped piece of paper. Attach the tie to the picture of the dad. Glue the picture on the front of a sheet of folded card.

- **D Display:** A full display could be made, using lots of the brightly-coloured ties and with the D daddy words.

Cross-curricular links

Literacy: Write a story map entitled 'My Daddy Through the Years', depicting the different activities or occasions the child has shared with their dad. Add pictures.

Music: Rewrite the lyrics to 'Grandad I Love You', replacing it with 'Daddy I Love You'. For example:

> Daddy I Love You
> Daddy I care
> Though you may be funny
> You still have no hair
> And one day when I'm older
> I'll look back and say
> Daddy I remember when you were grey!

RE/PSHCE: Read and share the poem below. Tea-stain sheets of paper to make them look like parchment and ask the children to write their own versions of the poem.

What Makes a Dad

> God took the strength of a mountain,
> The majesty of a tree,
> The warmth of a summer sun,
> The calm of a quiet sea,
> The generous soul of nature,
> The comforting arm of night,
> The wisdom of the ages,
> The power of the eagle's flight,
> The joy of a morning in spring,
> The faith of a mustard seed,
> The patience of eternity,
> The depth of a family need,
> Then God combined these qualities,
> When there was nothing more to add,
> He knew His masterpiece was complete,
> And so, He called it … Dad.

Independence Day

Whole-class starter

- On 4 July, you or an assistant could role-play Uncle Sam and enter the classroom in a red, white and blue outfit with stars, singing 'Happy birthday to us, Happy birthday to us, Happy birthday USA, Happy birthday to us!'

- Explain to the children that 4 July is the United States of America's birthday because in 1776 the United States became independent from Britain. The United States used to be made up of thirteen colonies, ruled by Great Britain's King George III. Americans decided they didn't like paying taxes to Great Britain and they wanted to be able to make their own decisions and not be told what to do by another country hundreds of miles away. However, King George was in no mood to talk and sent soldiers to deal with the situation. This caused the American Revolution in 1775. After a year of fighting, Americans decided to declare their country as independent. A committee was set up to draft a declaration of independence, and independence was finally proclaimed on 4 July 1776. Independence Day is now a national holiday in the United States, and is celebrated with family gatherings, barbecues, picnics, parades and fireworks.

Whole-class practical activity

- Play 'Strive for a Star'. Divide the class into two teams: red and blue. Pre-prepare questions about Independence Day and write them on laminated US flags (for example: How many colonies was the United States made up of? What was the name of Great Britain's King?). Display two American flags minus the stars. The object of the game is to win stars by answering questions about Independence Day. The team with the most stars at the end of the game is the winner.

Art and display

The following ideas offer different ways of creating and texturing the Stars and Stripes. They can be put together to make a Happy Birthday America card – with title letters made out of flags too.

- **American Flags:**
  - Finger-paint the United States flag.
  - On black card, using thick paint and glue spreader, create the American flag.
  - Collage the flag, using a variety of different types of paper.
- **American Collage Picture:** Using magazines and clip art pictures, create a collage of different United States landmarks.

- **American Star Art:** Using red, white and blue, create a background with chalk pastels. With felt-tipped pens, draw and colour a star based on the US flag's stars. Cut it out and glue on the background.
- **Whole-class Project:** Invite the children to work together to draw and use chalk pastels to create a United States montage. This can be the centre-piece of a display.
- **Famous Americans:** Choose an influential American figure, for example Abraham Lincoln, to draw and colour in the style of Picasso. The children draw in pencil and use felt tips to add colour.

Cross-curricular links

ICT: Use a website such as www.tagxedo.com to create a star-shaped word cloud full of words related to American Independence Day.

History: Research important figures linked to the time of US independence, including Samuel Adams, Benjamin Franklin, John Hancock, Patrick Henry, Thomas Jefferson, Paul Revere and George Washington.

History: Watch a movie linked to Independence Day, such as *1776* (1972), *Drums Along the Mohawk* (1939) and *Last of the Mohicans* (1992). For little ones, *Ben and Me* (1953) is an appropriate option.

Sports Day

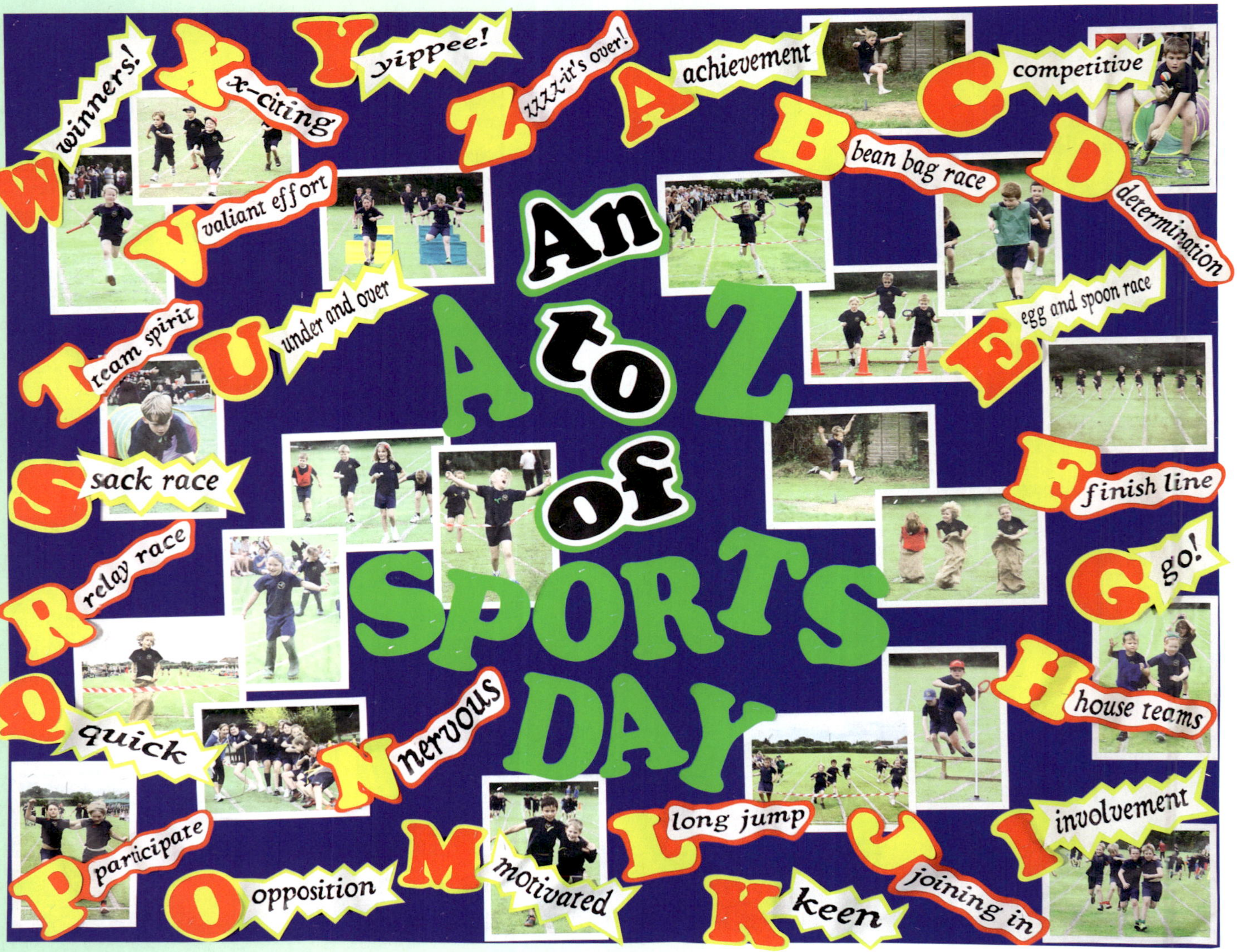

The A to Z of Sports Day display shows:

W winners! · Y yippee! · X x-citing · Z zzz...it's over! · A achievement · competitive · B bean bag race · C · D determination · valiant effort · team spirit · U under and over · egg and spoon race · E · sack race · F finish line · relay race · G go! · quick · house teams · H · participate · nervous · N · involvement · I · opposition · M motivated · L long jump · J joining in · K keen

An A to Z of Sports Day

Whole-class starter

- Pre-record children or adults talking about their Sports Day experiences. Aim to include a range of views, such as a love of Sports Day (e.g. the competiveness and hope to win) and a dread of Sports Day (e.g. dislike of an activity and disapproval of competitiveness). Discuss with the children why adults and children feel like this. Give the children a sticky note each and ask them to write down how they feel about Sports Day. Display the notes and encourage the children to read and discuss their views.

- Read and enjoy *Sports Day* by Nick Butterworth.

- Talk about how Sports Days are held at different times of the year in different countries. For example it is the summer in New Zealand in November or December so Sports Days are more likely to be held then, while in the UK they are more likely to be held in the UK's summer months of June or July.

Whole-class practical activity

- Discuss with the children the types of Sports Day that take place in different schools. Talk about the events that people organise for these days. Discuss how some Sports Days are non-competitive. Ask: *What does 'non-competitive' mean?* Some Sports Days are competitive. Ask: *What does this mean? What sort of Sports Day would you organise and why?*

- Tell the children that they are going to make an 'Alphabet of Sports Day'. Show the children each letter of the alphabet and as a class ask them to think of something that relates to Sports Day for each letter. For example: A = achievement, B = beanbag race, C = competitiveness, D = determination, E = egg and spoon race.

- Using an interactive whiteboard presentation, show the children a selection of photographs or pictures of children taking part in Sports Day events. Ask the children to write down what they think the people or children are thinking or saying in the images.

Art and display

Sports Day is a key event in the school calendar, and offers its own opportunities for art and display projects.

- **Sports Day Programme:** Design and make a Sports Day programme of events, which can be displayed for the whole school.

- **Sporty Alphabet:** Draw and colour an alphabet of sporting objects.

- **Alphabet Feelings:** The children can write a word for each letter of the alphabet about how sports day makes them feel.

- **Photo Display:** Create a Sports Day display after the event, using photographs of children, events and equipment, with the Alphabet Art.

Cross-curricular links

PE: Play 'Guess the Sports Object'. Place a selection of Sports Day objects in a bag. Blindfold the children. They must feel in the bag and guess as many objects as they can. Each object is worth 10 points. The child who guesses the most wins a medal.

PE: Make a 'Who Wants to Be a Millionaire?' Sports Day quiz to hold in the hall. Place a large A, B, C and D in each corner of the room. Prepare and then ask the children questions relating to Sports Day. For example: *What object carries the egg?* Give the children the answer options, such as: A = Spoon, B = Cup, C = Hand, D = Foot. The children must answer the question by running to one of the four corners.

PE: Invite the children to design and run their own Sports Day. Older children could work in groups to organise a sports day for the younger children in the school.

PE: Organise a Sports Day event for the winter. Include winter sports such as hockey, netball, rugby, football and basketball. This event is best matched to older Key Stage 2 children. Divide the children into teams. Each team plays each sport against each other. You could hold a Sports Day quiz and I-spy event too.

PSHCE: Discuss with children how they feel during Sports Day. Play 'Jingle Ball Feelings'. Pass the jingle ball around the circle. Each child must try and think of a word that describes how they feel about Sports Day. Increase the challenge by asking for words in alphabetical order, such as: A = anxious, B = brilliant, C= competitive, D= determined, E = eager, F = frightened, G = great, H= happy, I= included.

Pamplona: Running of the Bull

Whole-class starter

- Share with the children *The Story of Ferdinand* by Munro Leaf. If possible show enlarged images from the book while telling the story. The story explains how, while the other bulls ran, jumped and butted their heads together, Ferdinand preferred to sit and smell the flowers. Change the story and end it for now with Ferdinand being picked to take part in Pamplona's Running of the Bull festival.

- Explain that there is a festival in Spain to honour St Fermin – a saint believed to have been the son of a Roman senator, who became a Christian priest, and who died in AD303. He became the patron saint of Navarre, the area in which the festival is held. The San Fermin festival is centred in the town of Pamplona on 6 July with a firework from Pamplona's city hall. The next day there is a procession in which a statue of St Fermin is paraded through the streets. There is dancing and singing, and people dress up in costumes called *gigantes* and *cabezudos* (giants and big-heads). The Running of the Bulls takes place on 7 July and happens every day until 14 July. Hundreds of runners are pursued by six bulls and six steers along a street route that ends at the bullring in Pamplona. Before the run begins, the runners pray to Saint Fermin and ask for his protection. A firecracker tells the hundreds of runners that the bulls have been released, and the run begins. It is very dangerous and many people have been killed or injured.

Whole-class practical activity

- Show some images of the bull-run at Pamplona, such as the excited runners at the start, runners on the run, the crowd, the bulls, injured bulls, fallen runners, etc. Ask the children to work with a partner. Give each pair a few sticky notes and after showing each image ask each pair to think of one word to describe the feelings in each scene.

- Finally, go back to your version of *The Story of Ferdinand* and ask the children how they think Ferdinand would manage in the bull-run and what would happen to him. Together brainstorm endings to the story.

Art and display

The following project ideas will help create a display of different bulls using a variety of techniques.

- **Running Bull Picture:** Use chalk pastels to create a running bull picture.

- **Sketching Bulls:** Using sketching pencils, create an image of a bull. Use shading to emphasise the physical strength of the bull.

- **Spanish Flag Bull:** Draw an image of a bull using oil pastels. Add a striped background in red and yellow (the colours of the Spanish flag), to emphasise the link between bullfighting and Spain. An alternative is to use red and yellow for the bull and place it on a black background.

- **Scrunched Bull Art:** Scrunch an A3 sheet of paper very tightly, unfold and then using crayons draw and colour a black bull. Add a red and yellow background.

- **Silhouette Bull Art:** Watercolour a sunset background, then paint a black bull over it.

Cross-curricular links

Geography: Learn about Spain and the tradition of bullfighting. Create a pictorial map of Spain and its landmarks.

Literacy: Retell *The Story of Ferdinand*, adding a unique ending.

PSHCE: Debate the morality of bullfighting, including the pros and cons of it being entertainment.

Seasons

Autumn

Whole-class starter

- Prepare a selection of cards, one for each child, some with pictures or words that are related to autumn and some that are not, such as the words 'November', 'December' and 'Diwali' and a firework, conkers and Easter Bunny. Ask the children to sit in a circle. Explain that the year is divided up into four seasons and that they are going to learn all about autumn. Give each child a card and on a given signal ask the children to place the cards in either a hoop labelled 'Autumn' or a hoop labelled 'Not Autumn'. Discuss their choices.

Whole-class practical activities

- Send the children on a walk around the school to look for physical signs of autumn, such as leaves falling, conkers on the ground, squirrels scurrying and looking for nuts. Give them a laminated board with pictures of signs of autumn to look out for. Ask the children to tick any of the signs they see.

- Have a 'Mind Map Challenge'. Divide the children into groups of five. Place A2 sheets of paper around the classroom. Challenge the children to write as many things about autumn as they can remember. Give the children a set time to complete the task and encourage all the children to take turns to write on the mind map. This could be done as a race.

Art and display

The following project ideas are designed to make the most of the shapes, colours and other symbols of autumn.

- **Leaf Patterns:** Ask the children to draw around real leaves to make a leaf pattern. Paint the leaf pattern in autumn colours. You can use the artwork as the backing paper for a Signs of Autumn display.

- **Pen and Ink Squirrels:** Give the children a selection of squirrel pictures and encourage them to use pen and ink to draw their own squirrel.

- **Autumn Colours:** Using Paul Klee's painting style, create an autumn colour design with oil pastels.

- **Autumn Trees:** Using falling leaves as a focus create an autumn tree picture. Create the background with a bark rubbing. Crayon the tree on top of the background. Use an assortment of pre-cut circles to create a collage of falling leaves.

- **Autumn Scene:** Sponge a blue and green paint background. Charcoal a tree and add falling leaves made from tissue paper. Varnish the picture using a glue and water solution.

- **Hedgehog Art:** Using a blue background, add tissue paper to create a leaf effect. Use a piece of thick card to create a hedgehog shape, with pipe-cleaners for the spikes.

- **Still-life Conkers:** Gather and arrange conkers for children to draw. Use watercolours to paint still-life conker pictures.

- **Autumn Fruit:** Draw fruit shapes on white paper, using crayons to add colour and felt-tipped pens for the outline and seeds. Cut and stick the fruit shapes onto beige paper. Fill in the gaps by drawing and painting leaves using watercolours.

Cross-curricular links

Design and Technology: Make a hedgehog box.

Literacy: Create an autumn alphabet. Make a large zigzag book and place a letter of the alphabet on each page. Ask the children to draw or glue evidence of autumn for letters of the alphabet (e.g. A = apples, B = berries, C = conkers, D = dark nights, L = leaves).

Maths: Collect and count evidence of autumn. Ask the children to find ten conkers, four green leaves, seven acorns and three brown leaves, etc. Create an autumn counting table.

Winter

Whole-class starter

- Discuss with the children signs of winter. Create a mind map to show what the children know about winter

- Explain to the children that one of the most visible signs of winter is how trees change. Tell the children that all trees other than evergreen trees lose their leaves during winter and these are called deciduous trees. Take the children on a winter walk to look at deciduous trees. Look carefully at the tree shapes.

Whole-class practical activity

- Talk to the children about winter words. Sit the children in a circle and use a jingle ball (a blown-up ball with bells inside) – the children must roll the ball across the circle calling out a winter word. Focus on adjectives such as icy, misty, cold and chilly. Explain that these words are all adjectives and an adjective is a word that describes what something is like.

Art and display

The main project ideas here can be put together to make a Winter Wonderland display. An old-fashioned Georgian window display is another possibility.

- **Winter Wonderland:** Make the title with blue paper, backed onto silver. Add snow and icicle effects to give a wintry feel. Create a border using white paper cut out to give a snow and icicle effect.

- **Wintry Words:** Print winter words generated by the children onto A3 sheets. Cut them out giving them jagged edges for an icy effect. Back the words on silver paper.

- **Charcoal Winter Trees:** Sponge a background with blue paint on white A3 paper. Charcoal individual or multiple trees, or a whole winter tree scene. Mount the work on silver paper.

- **White Winter Trees:** Chalk pastel the background to create a wintry effect. Cut out a wintry tree from white paper and glue it onto the background. Mount the work on blue and silver paper.

- **Sewing Winter Trees:** Cut out a white circle of felt. Using black or brown thread, sew a simple winter tree onto it. For the best effect, use straight stitches. Mount the work on blue paper.

- **Winter Colour Snowflakes:** Using German artist Paul Klee's work for inspiration, create a chequered board effect using winter colours. Cut out the squares and glue them using a collage technique. Cut out a silver paper snowflake and glue onto the chequered background. Mount the work on silver paper.

- **Pen and Ink Window Display:** Research winter images from the past. Ask the children to reproduce a winter scene from the past on A3 paper using a pen and ink technique. Place their images in a window scene made from paper and card to depict the idea that the viewer is looking out from a Georgian-style window during wintertime.

Cross-curricular links

Geography: Research what winter is like in other parts of the world – in the far North such as Alaska, the Sahara and Australia. Identify countries where winter is similar or different to the children's country.

Literacy: Write a shape poem or calligram linked to winter. Create a bank of adjectives that could be used to write a descriptive poem about winter.

Music: Create a winter composition using winter words and percussion instruments that create winter sounds.

Spring

Whole-class starter

- Play a pre-prepared video of you in role as the King of Spring wearing a crown of daffodils. In the video explain that you are sending the class a message because it is nearly spring. Summer is the season when it's warmest and we wear cooler clothes and perhaps go to the beach; next it's autumn, a bit chillier and the leaves fall off the trees; then comes winter when it gets colder, and may snow; and after winter comes spring. Explain that spring usually begins about now and you can see lots of changes happening around you.

- The video continues with you in role asking the children to talk about what kind of changes they might expect to see in spring. Pre-record a period of spring music to follow, allowing the children time to discuss signs of spring. Still in role as the King, stop the discussion, asking: *Have you got some good ideas?* and set the challenge: *Tell me one change that you might see at springtime on the count of three: one, two, three …* . At this point the recording pauses to allow the children to feed back.

- Conclude the pre-recorded video with: *Excellent, excellent! Well I have a little present for you. There are some cards for you to have a look at.* (Give a pre-prepared laminated card to each pair of children with a picture of a spring item, e.g. daffodil, lamb, buds.) While the pairs discuss their card, the video concludes with the King talking through the things that they might see, and asking questions, such as: *Can you point to the yellow flower? This is called a daffodil and they are flowers you see in spring. Did you know that the bit in the middle is called a trumpet?*

Whole-class practical activity

- A parcel arrives from the King of Spring's palace. It's a pre-prepared recording of the King of Spring explaining that it's no good just staying indoors and talking about spring – it's better to get outside and see signs of spring for themselves, so their teacher will take them on a spring walk. On the walk they must search for the things the King has talked about. The King explains that he must go now as he needs to check the royal gardens himself for signs of spring too! Take the children on the walk with pre-prepared lists of spring signs for them to tick off.

Art and display

Here is a variety of ideas to explore spring through a selection of painting and collage techniques.

- **Giant King:** Paint and collage a giant King of Spring.

- **Spring Art:** Paint and collage large pictures of signs of spring – flowers, rabbits, baby animals, etc.

- **Spring Chick Art:** Using chalk pastels, create a spring chick in different poses.

- **Spring Garden:** Use tissue paper to create a spring garden picture.

- **Spring Word Art:** Ask the children to create the word SPRING using spring objects to form the letters. Draw and colour with pencil crayons.

Cross-curricular links

ICT: Create a spring-watch video or presentation using photographs taken on a spring walk.

Literacy: Learn about verbs and words ending in –*ing*.

Music: Listen to Vivaldi's 'Four Seasons' and then create a spring composition using percussion instruments.

Science: Create an indoor pond in a water tray in the classroom or put frogspawn in the school pond and watch the beginnings of the life cycle of frogs.

Summer

Board display featuring "S is for SUMMER SUN" with words: sweltering, burning, blistering, flaming, sizzling, warm, hot, flaming, boiling, baking, scorching, fiery, blazing

Whole-class starter

- Discuss with the children signs of summer. Create a mind map to show what the children know about summer time.

- Explain that one of the most noticeable signs of summer is the sun. Discuss with the children the impact of the sun during the summer months. How does it make us feel? Place a large yellow circle in the middle of the classroom. Give each child a sun-ray. Ask the children to write a word on the sun-ray that describes how they feel on a summer's day. Add this to the circle to make a large sun.

Whole-class practical activity

- Play 'Say it with a Sun'. Using an interactive whiteboard, show two images that placed together make a sun word, such as a picture of a sun and a hat (sunhat). Invite the children to guess the words and write them down on a whiteboard.

Art and display

Here are lots of different ideas for bringing the sun into your classroom.

- **Mosaic Sunshine:** Create an image of sunshine using mosaic-style shapes.

- **Chalk Pastel Sun:** Create a sunshine image using chalk pastels.

- **Aboriginal Sunshines:** Use Australian aboriginal art as an inspiration to paint sunshine pictures. Dab sunshine colours onto black card using cotton buds.

- **Fabric Sun:** Paint sunshine onto calico (or another white fabric) using oil pastels. Using a fabric dye, paint the background in blue. Use the couching technique to add detail with wool.

- **Sunny Rays:** Create a sunshine face collage on a blue background. Discuss what items could be used to depict sunshine rays (e.g. paint brushes, fingers, forks). Encourage the children to draw and use pencil crayons to illustrate their ideas.

- **Stitched Sun:** Create a padded sunshine using tissue and wadding. Use felt to create sun-rays. Add pen stitching for a sewn effect.

Cross-curricular links

Art: Create a whole-class sunshine using objects from around the school. Ask the children to gather as many yellow, red and orange objects as they can find to construct it.

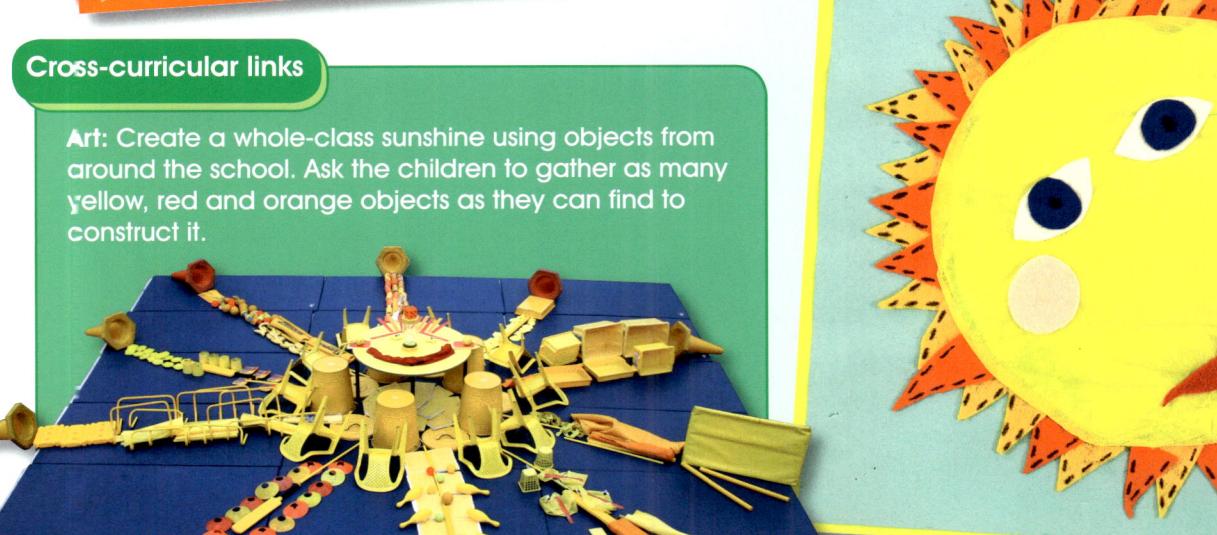

Summer Holidays

Whole-class starter

- Pack a suitcase with various items for a specific holiday destination (e.g. sun-cream and a swimming costume for a Caribbean holiday). Enter the class with the suitcase and explain that you have packed for your summer holiday. Ask the class to think about what they would put in their suitcase – would it be the same as what you have packed? Discuss with the children why it might be different. Explain that what you take with you often depends on where you are going. Reveal different items from your suitcase and ask the children to write on the interactive whiteboard what they think your destination might be, then discuss whether they are correct.

- Show the children other items for other destinations and ask them to guess the type of holiday each item would be for (e.g. a pair of walking boots and map for a mountainous walking holiday and a pair of ski boots for a skiing holiday).

Whole-class practical activities

- Play 'Pack Your Case and Go!'. Put the children in teams of five and pin large sheets of paper on the board. Give each team a pen. Line the children up for a relay-style race. On a given signal the children will race, one at a time, to write an item that a holidaymaker might pack. They race back and give the pen to the next person in the team who does the same. The children have three minutes to write as many holiday items as they can. Repeat for different types of holidays, such as a snorkelling holiday in the Red Sea, Egypt.

- Play 'I Packed in My Suitcase…'. Children take turns to say 'I packed in my suitcase…' (adding an item of their choice, e.g. a sun hat). Each child repeats the sentence, adding a new item each time. If a child makes a mistake they drop out.

- Create an alphabet of holiday destinations.

Art and display

Create a holiday classroom display to send the children off at the end of term.

- **Arcimboldo Art:** Using Arcimboldo's paintings for inspiration, the children create a face made up of items they might take on holiday to a chosen destination. Draw and chalk pastel their 'holiday heads'.

- **Postcard Art:** Choose a holiday destination and research its landmarks or attractions. Create a postcard picture that shows the type of holiday you could enjoy there. Draw and use pencil crayons or watercolours for the illustrations.

- **Holiday Word Art:** Ask the children to draw and colour objects related to a particular holiday, forming them into the word HOLIDAY.

- **Perspective Art:** Create a beach scene using chalk pastels. Focus on perspective and how umbrellas look from a distance.

Cross-curricular links

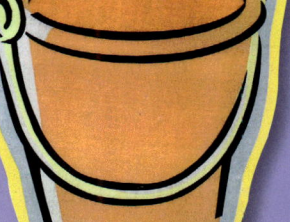

Design and Technology: Design and make a travel holiday game.

Drama: Set up a travel agent role-play area. Include items such as brochures, booking forms and a Bureau de Change.

Literacy: Ask the children to research a holiday destination and create a brochure advertising the location and/or activities.

Music: Play the song 'Summer Holiday' then rewrite the lyrics, for example:

> We're all going on a fishing holiday,
> No more talking for an hour or two,
> Still and quiet on my fishing holiday,
> Then the fish will come to you-ou-ou!
> For a bite and chew.

Remembrance Day

Whole-class starter

- In the week preceding Remembrance Day, read and share the story 'War Games' by Michael Foreman.

- Teach the children the facts about Remembrance Day in their own country. Use question words to help. For example: *Why does it happen? Who does it involve? Where does it take place? What do we do to celebrate Remembrance Day? When does it happen? How is Remembrance Day celebrated around the world?*

Whole-class practical activity

- Show a poignant image of a poppy field and World War I soldier or similar. Ask the children what it makes them think of. Give each child a poppy-shaped piece of paper and ask them to write a word or statement and place it on the picture. Invite the children to read each other's comments. Explain why the poppy became a symbol for Remembrance Day in European countries. (On the World War I battlefields of the Western Front, the poppies still flowered each year amongst the devastation, giving hope and symbolising life amongst death.)

- Use 'peace", "poppy', 'remembrance' or 'armistice' to write an acrostic poem depicting the children's thoughts. For example:

  People should never forget those who died to save us.
  Each year we should remember all those who fought so we could live.
  A poppy shows you have remembered.
  Caring is better than fighting.
  Everybody should want to live in peace and not in war!

Art and display

Poppies are a powerful image of the World War I, and a symbol of hope and peace. Different techniques can be used to create different feelings related to this topic.

- **Wartime Scene:** Paint a sunset background and add a poppy field with oil pastels. Collage a soldier and add crosses to depict wartime.

- **Collage Poppy Art:** On a blue background, use shades of red paper and material to create poppies.

- **Finger Painting Poppies:** Paint a poppy field using fingers only!

- **Remembrance Scene:** Use a variety of art mediums to create a remembrance poppy field. Sponge the background, then add a collage of crosses and poppies.

- **Watercolour Poppies:** Watercolour a poignant poppy scene.

Cross-curricular links

Design and Technology: Make a card poppy, then attach a cross, made from two lollipop sticks. Plant in a planter and create a class Remembrance Garden.

History: Research the significance of the poppy as the symbol of Remembrance Day. Discuss wars relevant to your country. For example in the United Kingdom you could discuss World War I and II, the Falklands War and the war in Afghanistan.

PSHCE: Discuss with the children: What is better, peace or war?

Ramadan and Eid al-Fitr

Whole-class starter

- Tell the children that they are going to learn about the religion of Islam. Explain that people who follow this religion are known as Muslims. Invite any Islamic children to explain or describe elements of their religion and its traditions. Share some facts with the children about Islamic mosques and how on the top of every mosque there is a crescent moon, which is the symbol of Islamic countries. Their name for God is Allah and their day of worship is Friday. Muslims pray five times a day; they wash before praying; and pray towards the direction of Mecca. Explain that there are five obligations (duties) one must live by as a Muslim, that are often called the Five Pillars of Islam.

Whole-class practical activity

- Tell the children that the festival of Ramadan is one of the Five Pillars of Islam and that today they are going to learn all about Ramadan. Tell them to listen to statements about the festival and decide if they are true or false. Divide the children into two teams and encourage them to discuss which statements are correct. If they guess correctly they collect a letter from the word 'Ramadan'. The first team to win the letters to make the word 'Ramadan' wins the game. (Examples of true statements: Ramadan is the ninth month of the Islamic calendar; Ramadan is a month of fasting; Ramadan ends with a celebration called Eid al-Fitr.)

- Discuss with the children how Muslims believe in doing good for others. Kindness and charitable gifts are a big part of the festival of Ramadan. Give each child a sheet of paper in the shape of a crescent moon. Ask them to write on it an act of kindness that they have already done that day. Display the crescents on a board so that the children can share their acts of kindness as a class.

Art and display

The beautiful shapes of a mosque and of a crescent moon, can be used to great effect in creating a Ramadan display.

- **Collaged Mosque:** Using lots of brightly-coloured wrapping paper, cut out and collage a picture of a mosque.

- **Crescent Moon Art:** Create a deep blue background using ripped tissue paper. On a white crescent moon, using a blue felt-tipped pen, create Muslim-style patterns. Stick the crescent moon onto the blue background.

- **Mosque Art:** On black card use white chalk to sketch a mosque scene.

- **Mix Medium Mosque:** Create a purple and white background using chalk pastels. With black paint, add an image of a mosque.

- **Thick Paint Mosque:** Using a range of thick paints and a glue spreader create a mosque scene.

Cross-curricular links

PSHCE: Create a Ramadan highway code using symbols. You can find examples on the internet by searching 'Ramadan Highway Code'.

PSHCE: Create a good deed jar for the classroom. Children write on cards good deeds they could do in the classroom. Each day a different child picks a good deed card and carries out the deed.

Science: Cut out phases of the Moon for a story wheel showing the cycle of the Moon's phases.

Mother's Day

Throughout this topic remember that some children in the class may have an absent father or mother, or there may be sensitive issues linked to either or both parents. Adjust the lesson accordingly.

Whole-class starter

- Mother's Day is celebrated in several countries around the world on different dates. In a large number of countries, including the USA and Australia, Mother's Day is celebrated on the second Sunday in the month of May, but in many other countries Mother's Day is celebrated at a different time of the year. Whatever the date, the spirit is the same everywhere. All around the world children thank their mothers for their care and love.

- Read and enjoy *Five Minutes' Peace* by Jill Murphy. What is the story about? What is the message in the story?

- Discuss the link between the book and Mother's Day. Ask the children who thinks their mum deserves a special day. What can we do for our mums on Mother's Day to show them that we care?

Whole-class practical activity

- Listen to the song 'No Charge' by Tammy Wynette. Discuss the lyrics. Make a list of all the things we should thank our mums for.

Art and display

Here are two different themes that can be followed to create different displays. One focuses on 'mum' – the creations can be used for Mother's Day cards too. The other uses Picasso's Mother and Child painting for inspiration.

- **Teapot Art:** Give each child a teapot-shaped piece of paper. Add a bright coloured pattern with oil pastels.

- **Cup Cake Art:** Give each child a square of brightly coloured wrapping paper. Make a cup cake out of a concertina of card. Create the top of the cake using tissue paper and add shiny paper for the cherry.

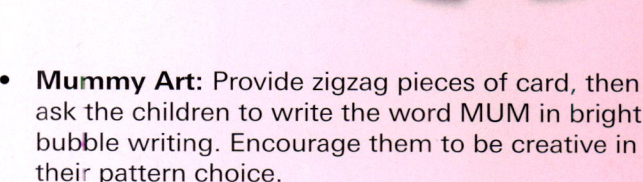

- **Mummy Art:** Provide zigzag pieces of card, then ask the children to write the word MUM in bright bubble writing. Encourage them to be creative in their pattern choice.

- **Mother and Child:** Use the blue Mother and Child painting by Picasso as a stimulus and invite the children to draw their own interpretation of the painting. Add colour with a range of blues. Children can also create their own Mother and Child image, using felt-tipped pens and a brush stroke technique.

- **Sculpture:** Sculpt a clay mother and child.

Cross-curricular links

History of Art: Research and discuss the life of Picasso.

Literacy: Write an acrostic poem using the word 'Mum', 'Mummy' or 'Mother'.

Literacy: Share a selection of books based on mothers being marvellous (e.g. *My Mum is Fantastic* by Nick Butterworth and *Me and My Mum* by Alison Ritchie and Alison Edgson).

Textiles: Make a wall hanging. Sew the word 'Mum', 'Mummy' or 'Mother' with fabric onto a piece of hessian. Place dowelling across the top for hanging.

Harvest Celebrations

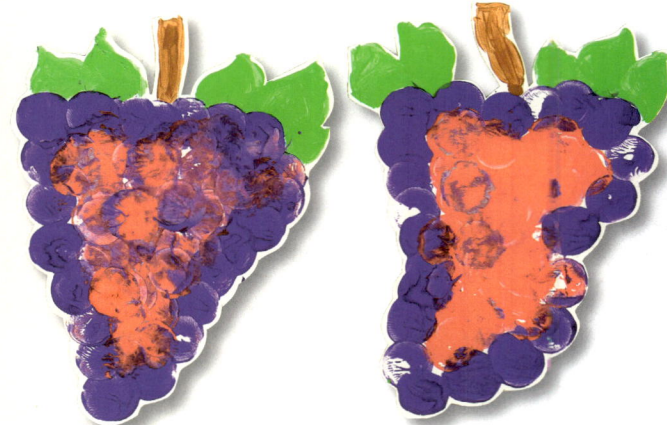

Whole-class starter

- If possible, role-play Farmer Giles and arrive in the classroom pushing a wheelbarrow containing a selection of items that represent Harvest festivals in various countries, such as:
  - moon cakes (China)
  - a corn dolly (Europe)
  - a bowl of rice (Japan)
  - a bunch of grapes (Australia)
  - a branch from a tree (Mexican Tree of Life)
  - an apple (American Thanksgiving).
- Tell the children that harvest time celebrates the gathering of crops at the end of the summer to provide food for everyone to eat. It is all about sharing and today they are going to share their knowledge of harvest celebrations, not just in this country but in countries all around the world. Show the children each item in your wheelbarrow, explaining what they represent to different countries.

Whole-class practical activity

- Using the word 'harvest', create a class acrostic poem that describes the traditions of different harvest times around the world.
- Play the 'Splatting Harvest Game'. Create a board with pictures linked to the different harvest festivities and traditions around the world. Divide the children into two teams. A player from each team stands with their back to the board, holding a giant fly-swatter. The teacher asks a question or gives the children a clue or statement. The children must quickly turn and splat the correct picture that relates to the question, clue or statement.

Art and display

Harvest is very different in different parts of the world. The following project ideas use a selection of techniques to make images for a 'World Harvest' display.

- **Harvest Picture:** Paint and use collage to create giant pictures of fruit, vegetables and corn dollies. Back onto black paper and arrange to represent a harvest festival offering.

- **Mexican Tree Art:** Draw a Mexican Tree of Life using felt-tipped pens for details and colour. Encourage children to draw things that represent important things in their lives.

- **Grape Art:** Let children study bunches of grapes, then watercolour their own images, or print bunches of grapes using thick paint and a circular template.

- **Apple Art:** Using watercolour pencils, draw and colour still-life apple pictures.

- **Apple Collage:** Create apple collages using apple-coloured paper. The children cut out apple shapes and use an overlapping collage technique.

- **Red and Green Apples:** Use chalk pastels to create a picture of a collection of red and green apples.

- **African Mask:** Using thick card and acrylic paint, work in groups to create an African harvest mask.

- **Moon Festival Art:** Paint a moon with chalk pastels, cut it out and glue it onto a blue paper background. Create a Chinese moon goddess with pencil crayons. Cut out and add to the background.

- **Colourful Cow Art:** Give each child a cow-shaped piece of paper. Using oil pastels create bright colourful patterns on the cow shape.

Cross-curricular links

Design and Technology: Bake moon cakes or your own bread corn dolly.

Design and Technology: Design and make a Chinese lantern.

Dance: Create a harvest dance based on the harvest-time Kassa dance, performed in East Guinea. It tells the story of good and bad ghosts battling to keep harvest successful.

Literacy: Retell traditional harvest-time stories from around the world, such as *The Corn Dolly*, *Johnny Appleseed*, *Kimoto and the Rice Harvest*.

Literacy: Write the words 'world harvest' on the board and challenge the children to make as many harvest-linked words as possible using the letters from 'world harvest' (e.g. share, love, earth).

Songkran: Water Festival (pages 38–39)

Valentine's Day (pages 24–25)